Unexplained Scotland

CW01551441

Martin R. Shaw

"The more unknowable the mystery,
the more beautiful it is."
-David Lynch

Contents

Preface. i

Introduction. iii

Aleister Crowley & Boleskine House. 1

Bonnybridge & Zalus 11

The Grey Man. 17

The Glasgow Witches. 23

The Wizard of Yester. 29

A75: The Ghost Road 33

The Blairgowrie UFOs 39

The Trouble at Ringcroft. 45

The Flannan Lighthouse Mystery. 53

Netta & Iona 61

The Livingston Encounter. 69

The Egyptian Bone 75

The East Kilbride Goblin 81

The A70 Abduction 85

The Monster of Glamis 91

The Bargarran Possession 97

Morag: The Monster of Loch Morar 103

The Calvine UFO Photo 109

Robert Gordon & The Devil 115

Edinburgh's Tiny Coffins 119

The Gorbals Vampire 123

The Brahan Seer 127

Mary King's Close 133

The Gurning Man 139

Nessie's Exorcism 145

Epilogue 151

Acknowledgements 153

About The Author 155

Bibliography 157

Preface

I like to think of this book and the stories told in it as a David Bowie mixtape.

Sure, maybe you've heard some of the classics like The Gorbals Vampire, The Livingston Encounter, and The Gurning Man ("Changes", "Life On Mars?", and "Ziggy Stardust") but the mix also includes lesser known deep cuts that aren't nearly as popular as they should be, like Nessie's Exorcism, Bonnybridge & Zalus, and A75: The Ghost Road ("Watch That Man", "Somebody Up There Likes Me", and "Always Crashing In The Same Car"), and even one that should probably be left out of the mix but is so strange and surreal that it has to be heard to be believed; The East Kilbride Goblin ("The Laughing Gnome").

Even if you're familiar with some of the stories in this book, I can guarantee you haven't heard them told as they are here. Rather than a stuffy retelling of events in a dry textbook style, I've retold them in a unique way. I've injected my own brand of humour into the more fantastical and strange elements of the stories, presented some of my own theories, asked questions no one else has the guts to ask, and generally tried to make each tale as entertaining as possible.

If you know every one of these stories of the mysterious, the supernatural and the unexplained, you're still going to get an entirely original, fun-filled and possibly baffling retelling.

Despite the fun I hope you're going to have reading these stories, they all have some basis in truth. In each of these stories, one or more people saw or experienced something strange.

I believe in the paranormal. I believe that every one of these stories has at least a sliver of truth to them. Between the jokes, puns, and uncounted pop culture references, the original facts (or supposed facts) still remain in there. In each case, someone experienced something terrifying. But what is terrifying to a person at the time, when retold can sound weird, ridiculous, unbelievable and even hilarious. Just because these subjects are serious, it doesn't mean we can't have some fun.

So here it is; *Unexplained Scotland.* A book that I humbly hope will make you laugh, cringe, turn all your lights on out of fear, think about the very nature of reality, and consider your place in the universe. Most of all though, what I want to get across is that these subjects can be fun. It doesn't have to be seriously examined, bunked and debunked, and debated over social media. At least not all the time. Sometimes we can just look at it, and have a laugh. No matter whether you believe in all this stuff or not, it's undeniable that a lot of it is straight up silly. The high strangeness in a lot of cases cannot be retold with a straight face, and I don't attempt to.

This is a book for the Mulders and the Scullys, the sceptics and the true believers.

As long as they have a sense of humour.

Introduction

Scotland is weird.

Inside its small 30,000 square miles are contained more paranormal encounters, legends, folklore, and tales of the unexplained than most countries several times its size. You cannot enter a city, town, or village without some ancient legend or modern myth being told to you. Dark beasts stalk the woods and mountains, ghosts haunt everywhere from farms to theatres to subways, the lochs are riddled with monsters, witches and warlocks cast curses and summon monstrous minions, occultists try to conjure the devil himself, UFOs attack ordinary people in broad daylight, and much, much more.

But why is this? Is it due to the age of the country? Scotland is so ancient that it makes many larger countries like the United States look like newborns by comparison. From Druids to Saxons, Scotland has been occupied by a great number of peoples all bringing their own beliefs, religions and superstitions to the country. Could this mishmash of mysticism have stirred something up that has made Scotland just a little bit more unusual than most other places in the world?

Or could it be that Scotland has always been a strange place, even before anyone set foot here? Throughout the world you find places where high strangeness seems to be the normal. Places like Skinwalker

Ranch,

The Bermuda Triangle, Point Pleasant and Twin Peaks. Places like these, John Keel, author of *The Mothman Prophecies*, speculates are areas where the veil between this world and some other, hidden, unknown world is thin. In these areas strange creatures are seen, UFOs are spotted, poltergeists torment locals, and things are rarely as they seem. While these areas are relatively small, usually no bigger than a town, is it possible that the entirety of Scotland could be on the thin end of the veil? Inside Scotland itself are also individual paranormal hotspots, perhaps while the veil is even thinner, or has been munched by moths (or mothmen).

I could go on forever about the possible reasons that Scotland has so much weirdness about it, and maybe you'll form some theories of your own by the end of this book. The important thing is that Scotland is weird. Strangely though, most of Scotland's weird tales remain fairly unknown, even to the people who live here. Ask most people about the paranormal and the unknown in Scotland and they'll likely tell you about Loch Ness' most famous resident and that'll be it. Scotland, I believe, has encounters that could rival and even surpass some of the most worldwide famous UFO encounters, cryptid sightings, demonic possessions and tales of the occult.

By the end of this book I hope you'll agree with me, and see that Scotland has far more weirdness to offer than just good old Nessie.

Aleister Crowley & Boleskine House

Aleister Crowley: the most famous occultist of all time.

If you haven't heard of Crowley, you have certainly felt his influence in pop culture. He's inspired countless hard rock and heavy metal songs, perhaps most famously Ozzy Osbourne's 'Mr. Crowley', but his influence is felt everywhere in music, from Iron Maiden to David Bowie to The Beatles. He became the archetypal "evil occultist" figure for film, television and literature; famously inspiring the villain in the novel *The Devil Rides Out*, and subsequent Hammer Horror film adaptation. This portrayal was hardly surprising as he was known in the press as "The Wickedest Man In The World" and "A Man We'd Like To Hang".

In the world of the occult he is still a prominent figure. His books are still sold and read today, he still inspires many to have an interest in the subject, and his own occult philosophy still has a great number of followers. Crowley has been the subject of thousands of books, documentaries, podcasts, webseries, and just about every piece of media imaginable. Every piece of his life has been pored over by scholars, followers, and detractors, but it's one specific point of his life that may be the most interesting and bizarre: his time in Scotland's Boleskine House *and* what happened to his abode before and after he vacated it.

Origin Of The Beast

Aleister Crowley's life was an unusual one from the get-go. He was born to wealthy parents in Warwickshire, England in 1875. Both of his parents were devout Christians, which was something he would rebel against from a young age. It seemed the only part of Christianity he liked was the Book of Revelation. He was obsessed with the imagery of the rapture, the end times, and demons walking the earth. He enjoyed it so much that he adopted one of his many nicknames from its pages. He became known as 'The Great Beast 666'. Throw up those metal horns.

While he was in Cambridge College he began writing poetry. These caused controversy for very different reasons. Some were Satanic, causing a moral panic with the religious crowd. Others were pornographic, and were so vulgar it offended just about everyone who read them. With a poetry book titled *White Stains*, I think you'll thank me if I don't go into too much detail about the content of these poems. It was also during his time in college that he made an early trip to Scotland. He travelled to Glasgow, and swiftly caught gonorrhoea from a prostitute.

After college, he was put in touch with the Hermetic Order of The Golden Dawn by a friend while discussing his interest in alchemy; the mystical art of transforming matter. The Golden Dawn was a magical society dedicated to the study and practice of the occult, the paranormal, and magick (spelt with a 'ck' rather than just a 'c' so you know it's the real deal). Crowley took to this group with an unprecedented enthusiasm, and within two years he had climbed the ranks of the group with incredible speed.

Crowley wanted to further his magical training however, and was feeling held back by the rules and hierarchy of The Golden Dawn. He chose to perform a ritual from the Book of Abramelin; a grimoire written by an Egyptian mage in the 1400s. Not only had no one attempted anything from this book in centuries, its preface specifically tells the reader *not* to attempt anything within it; a pre-warning similar to the introduction to *Jackass*. Crowley, never one to follow rules or listen to warnings, decided to try it anyway, much like hundreds of teenagers after seeing Johnny Knoxville attach fireworks to his roller skates... and with similar results.

To perform his chosen ritual he needed a location with very specific specifications. He needed a home that would provide enough solitude and privacy for intense and lengthy meditation. The home needed a North facing door. The door needed to open onto a terrace covered in sand. At the end of the terrace there needed to be a lodge in which evil spirits could be summoned, gathered, and bound.

Crowley searched long and hard for the perfect location, believing he would perhaps find it in the Lake District. After being unsuccessful here, he decided to look elsewhere. This brought him back to Scotland.

Enter Boleskine

Along the shores of Loch Ness, famous for a different type of monster, Crowley found the perfect place: Boleskine House.

Boleskine already had a strange history before Crowley even set foot in it. On this location was originally Boleskine Parish, built in the 13th century. In the 1600's it was said that the minister of the parish was given the job of killing zombies raised from a local graveyard by an evil necromancer. A priest's duties used to be *very* different.

The parish later, according to legend, burned down with its entire congregation inside, killing them all. Whether this was also the work of the evil warlock or just an unattended kettle is unknown. Boleskine House was built on this same land, to be used as a hunting lodge in 1760.

This was the building that Crowley came to. It had a North facing door that led onto a terrace that went straight to a lodge. As for the sand required for the ritual, Crowley could just take some from the nearby Loch. Crowley was so sure that this was his perfect location that in 1899 he, being the master negotiator, paid twice the asking price and moved in.

Soon after arriving at Boleskine, Crowley started to prepare for his ritual. The purpose of the ritual was to invoke his guardian angel and obtain mystical knowledge from it. The knowledge given would result in Crowley being gifted more power as a magician and a greater understanding of the occult. Performing the ritual was to be no easy task. To begin with, Crowley had to abstain from sex, drugs, and alcohol for six months. No easy feat, as these were three of Crowley's favourite things in the whole wide world.

Crowley then had to meditate before sunrise and after sunset. I imagine this was also a challenge as I can't picture Crowley as a morning person. While abstaining and meditating, he also had to spend this time in near total isolation. Very hard for a man who famously loved attention.

Once this initial part of the ritual was completed, the difficulty level increased with the next step: Crowley had to summon the Kings and Dukes of Hell.

This included Baal; who had the head of a man, the head of a cat, and the head of a frog. Purson; who appears as a man with the face of a lion, riding a bear, and Amdusias; who is a man with claws and the head of a unicorn. The purpose of this was to bind the demonic Kings and Dukes to the lodge on the property, removing their negative influence from his life. These demons would also grant Crowley certain powers such as levitation, the ability to predict the future, invisibility, and the incredibly useful power to bend trees at will, to name just a few. Along with these demons, he'd also be summoning their personal legions of lesser demons who served them.

During his time preparing for and performing the ritual, locals became curious as to what Crowley was doing in Boleskine.

His reputation certainly preceded him and the townsfolk knew the man who had just moved into their neighbourhood was a black magician, an occultist, a sexual deviant, and "The Wickedest Man in The World." It wasn't long until tales regarding Crowley's activities in Boleskine started flying wild. Rumours of unnamed locals getting a look through a window and seeing Crowley leading Satanic black masses, performing evil occult rituals with a legion of cloaked disciples, and more scenes straight out of a Dennis Wheatley novel quickly spread through the area like wildfire.

Given Mr. C's history and reputation, these rumours aren't totally ridiculous. However, judging by his dedication to the isolation needed to perform his ritual I think it's safe to assume these rumours were just tall tales made up in the local pub.

That's not to say that strange things weren't happening in and around Boleskine House though. By Crowley's own accounts of his time in the house, he was perhaps too successful in summoning the Kings and Dukes of Hell to come and live in his lodge. He puts the weird events of this time down to his fantastic success, and would even admit that things did get "out of hand". Something of an understatement.

Crowley claims a workman on his land became deranged and attempted to murder him. His coachman, a sober man, got drunk and tried to kill his own family. The two children of Crowley's housekeeper died suddenly and abruptly. Perhaps the strangest of all was when Crowley absentmindedly noted down some demons' names on a butcher's receipt that he mistook for a scrap piece of paper. Later, the butcher he received the receipt from slipped while cutting meat for a customer, severed an artery, and bled to death.

Locals became so afraid of Crowley that some eventually tried to win his favour by leaving a homemade, illegal bottle of whisky on his doorstep. They believed Crowley had control over the forces he had summoned, when he was really just letting them run amok. He kept the whiskey to enjoy later, though.

Crowley had almost completed the ritual: he had abstained and meditated for six months, he had summoned the Kings and Dukes of Hell and bound them to the lodge. He decided it was finally time to take the final step and summon his guardian angel. As he was preparing to do this though, he was suddenly called back to The Golden Dawn. The magical society was experiencing infighting and was on the verge of imploding and tearing itself apart. Crowley abandoned the ritual and quickly travelled back to The Golden Dawn to try and help save his group, and to demand the promotion he was sure he rightly deserved.

Crowley returned to Boleskine a couple of times over the next several years, but never for very long. Eventually, he just didn't come back. It seemed like he had abandoned the idea of contacting his guardian angel in the house (or had just forgotten why he bought the property in the first place). He never finished the ritual there. He never banished the demons he summoned. He just left them for the next owner to deal with, like an old couch.

Crowley Continues

After abandoning Boleskine, Crowley would eventually leave the Golden Dawn and create his own magical and occult society/philosophy known as Thelema.

He set up an Abbey in Sicily where he and several of his followers, known as Thelemites, lived. After learning of the sordid activities that took place in Thelema Abbey, and the death of one of the Thelemites due to a liver infection, the dictator Mussolini deported Crowley. The Abbey closed down shortly after. How bad do you have to be to make *Mussolini* kick you out?

Crowley would eventually meet his guardian angel, without having to go through the whole bother of summoning it, in Egypt. It introduced itself as Aiwass and curiously looked very similar to the modern popular description of an alien; grey coloured skin, large head, and big black eyes. Aiwass would dictate to Crowley what would be released as *The Book of the Law*, and would become an essential part of Thelema.

Crowley eventually died a penniless drug addict in a nursing home in England in 1947. He never got to see the massive influence he would have in pop culture that began just over a decade later; bummer - he'd have loved it!

Demons & Rockstars

Although Crowley had left Boleskine, the story of the property would continue without him.

Boleskine lay empty for some years until Crowley finally sold it in 1913. Shortly after the First World War, Boleskine (or rather the land Boleskine was built on) was involved in a scam involving shares in a non-existent pig farm. Whether this was the result of Crowley's magick, or the demons he summoned, is up for debate.

In 1965 Boleskine had its next proper resident. An army major moved in, but soon after shot himself in Crowley's old bedroom. Next, a married couple moved in. The husband broke up with his wife and moved out after only one month. The wife was blind, and was left to wander around her new home unable to see a thing.

In 1970 Boleskine had its next, and perhaps most famous, owner. Jimmy Page, guitarist for *Led Zeppelin*, bought Boleskine House. Page was a big fan of the occult and Crowley in particular. On the vinyl for the album *Led Zeppelin III*, a phrase from Crowley's Thelema can be found etched into the very wax. In the middle run-off, the words "Do What Thou Wilt" can be seen. Page also owned an occult bookshop in London called Equinox which stocked rare and original books by famous occultists, and contained more than a couple of pieces by Aleister himself. At one point in his life, Page even owned the world's second largest collection of Crowley's books.

Being such a fanboy of Crowley, it's no surprise that he jumped at the chance to own Boleskine. He intended to return it to the condition it would have been in while Crowley lived there. This was to be no small job however, as in the years it was unoccupied Boleskine had fallen into disrepair and required a lot of work.

Still, the rockstar took on the task and began to plan the work needed to return the house to its former glory. Outside of occult reasons, Page also thought Boleskine would make a good holiday home and an inspiring place to write new music. This was something he would soon double back on. He only visited a handful of times, and was reportedly put off the property's holiday home potential when he heard a ghostly severed head rolling across the floor. Perhaps the demons took offence to *Stairway To Heaven* being played in their new domain, and sought to scare the guitarist out of the building like some real life *Scooby-Doo* villains.

Page decided to ask his friend Malcolm Dent to act as a caretaker for Boleskine while he was away on tour/afraid to return due to disembodied heads rolling about. Dent, doing not much of anything else at the time, said "Yeah, sure, why not?". He ended up staying for two decades.

Soon after moving in, Dent started to repair Boleskine. He worked on the interior which had been ravaged by a fire at some unknown point in its disuse, and landscaped the surrounding area which had become overgrown and jungle-like. Dent was a sceptic towards all things paranormal, but soon after starting his work on Boleskine things began to happen that he couldn't explain. He would hear strange noises in the rooms and halls that would stop when he went to investigate them, then start again after he left. Doors would slam around the house during the night for no reason. He would go into rooms and find carpets, rugs and other items piled up in the centre. He also experienced what he called the "most terrifying night of his life" in Boleskine.

He was awoken one night to strange sounds outside his bedroom door. As he listened, the sounds seemed to get louder and closer to his room. He described the sounds as a grunting and scraping, like they were coming from a large wild animal. Dent stayed up all night, too terrified to open his door. He was thinking some sort of wolf or wild boar had somehow gotten into the house. When the morning came, the noises stopped and Dent dared to look outside his bedroom door. There was nothing there, and there were no signs that anything had been there before. And it wasn't just Dent experiencing weird things at Boleskine. A friend of his, while staying over, claimed she was attacked by some sort of devil. None of this ever seemed to bother Dent though. Whenever strange things would happen, he would say "That's just Aleister doing his thing."

The only thing that did seem to bother Dent were the constant visitors to the property who were interested in Led Zeppelin or Crowley, proving that classic rock fans and occult nerds are far more annoying than any demon or ghost.

Boleskine Lives On

Page eventually sold Boleskine in 1992 and Dent moved out. The property was bought and sold a few times, usually to be used as a guesthouse or B&B. In 2015, while its new owners were out, the property caught fire. 60% of the building was destroyed and Boleskine was rendered uninhabitable.

A few years later a foundation bought what remained of Boleskine and planned to rebuild it. That was until 2019, when it caught fire *again*. Currently Boleskine is in a state of repair. The plans seem to be to reopen it for tourists, and perhaps even allow guests to stay. There are even rumours that it might lean into its occult history. While this is an appealing notion to modern Thelemites, fans of the occult, and dark tourists, whether or not it's a good idea is up for debate.

If the Kings and Dukes of Hell are still bound to Boleskine House, I'm sure they will appreciate the new company after so long alone. But will they sit quietly and play nice with their new visitors, or will they return to wreaking the same havoc they did as when Crowley summoned them? Surely the influx of occultists visiting will result in them performing rituals. Rituals which might stir up the old demons.

Boleskine House and the land it's built on seems destined for the paranormal.

From zombie attacks, to congregation killing fires, to Crowley summoning the forces of hell, to the more recent blazes, it seems like this is one of those places on the thin part of the veil between here and some other dimension where the supernatural dwells. Is it pure coincidence that this is where Crowley chose to perform his Abramelin ritual? A house that matched his very specific needs, while also having such a bizarre history?

Is it possible that Crowley was drawn to this place by whatever entity or entities dwelled on the land, in the knowledge that Crowley's ritual would open the veil between our world and theirs even more, allowing them more power here? A plan that went awry when Crowley suddenly had to depart, leaving these entities, or King and Dukes of Hell, in a kind of limbo bound to Boleskine House? Were they made more powerful by the ritual, but trapped by its abandonment and unable to leave the property?

Were they attempting to use Crowley for their own means, only to be betrayed and left in an old, empty house? Were they left for decades in a strange halflife, only able to torment and terrify the residents who dwelled there, waiting for someone to return who could finish the ritual and release them? Was it them who tried to burn the place down in an attempt to escape their imprisonment?

Is it also a coincidence that sightings of the Loch Ness Monster increased drastically after Crowley attempted his ritual? Could Nessie be one of the demons summoned by the occultist? Or could it be that Crowley's magick just unlocked the paranormal prison it was locked in by Saint Columba over one thousand years prior?

Whatever the future holds for Boleskine House and the land it stands on, I think it's safe to assume that more strangeness is to come. If the plans to rebuild and reopen go ahead this time, this might be the first guest house with the rules:

"No noise after 10, No smoking, No summoning the forces of Hell".

Bonnybridge & Zalus

A mass of UFO sightings in the same area over a short period of time reported by multiple witnesses, also known as a "flap" (stop laughing.), is a phenomenon that has happened many times throughout history.

From ancient times when hundreds of people reported seeing moving stars in the night sky, to more recent years when many see unknown crafts and objects flying above everywhere from towns, cities, oceans, motorways, and just about everywhere you could think of. Why certain places suddenly become areas that UFOs seem to take a particular interest in is unknown, but just about every country has at least one location that has at one time or another become practically invaded by strange crafts.

Scotland, of course, is no exception.

The Flap Begins

In the early 1990's the small Scottish town of Bonnybridge became a hotbed of UFO activity.

The first incident occurred one night in January of 1992, when a Mr. James Walker was playing against his name by driving home. Above the road he saw an unusual cross formation of lights which he initially dismissed as stars, despite their brightness and odd pattern. As he drove further, he looked back at these 'stars' in his rear view mirror. As he did, he saw the lights rearrange themselves into a triangle shape. Something, he rightly noted, that stars were not known to do.

Later, in March of the same year, at around 7pm, the Slogett family were slogging it towards Bonnybridge. As they were walking, Mr. Steven Slogett spotted an odd ball of light in the sky. As he pointed it out to his family, the ball of light suddenly started descending and landed in a nearby field. They decided against investigating the strange ball, thinking that it might be dangerous; perhaps fallen debris from a plane or an extraterrestrial egg with a parasitic alien lifeform inside, and continued their walk. As they continued on their way to Bonnybridge they were all of a sudden stopped by a football sized ball of blue light hovering over the road in front of them. As they got closer to the ball, a small hatch opened on its side and a howling sound came from within. The family was blinded by a bright flash and ran the rest of the way to Bonnybridge. From their home, they could still see the light from the strange object, as did many other people.

Flapping Intensifies

There were many more strange encounters around this time, some even photographed or videoed with the traditional blurry and out of focus quality we've come to expect of UFO evidence. However, it wasn't the encounters themselves that were particularly of interest; but rather the number of them.

Local councillor Billy Buchanan claimed that he had received over 400 reports of UFO activity from his constituents, a large number considering Bonnybridge's population of just 5,500. It was this volume of reports that attracted the attention of the media. As reporters from all over the country descended on the town and locals' fear was rising, Billy Buchanan felt it was his duty to find answers. To calm and educate the public, Buchanan called a town meeting in January 1993. Almost 300 people turned up to hear a lecture on the UFO phenomenon from an expert on the subject. Sadly, the hypnotist who specialised in unearthing alien abduction memories didn't show up.

As the encounters continued, Buchanan received a mysterious visitor who remains anonymous to this day. The visitor was a man who claimed to be a spokesperson for an alien entity known as Zalus (or was Zalus the spokesperson himself?). Zalus was part of the Council Of Nine, which was something like an intergalactic UN or The Federation from *Star Trek*. This visitor told Buchanan that Zalus had an important message for the people of Earth. A message regarding Earth's role in the evolution of the universe; pretty important stuff!

Upon receiving this message via Zalus' anonymous messenger, Buchanan called another town meeting to share the news with the people of Bonnybridge. This went about as well as you'd expect. The locals did not take it seriously, and the press even less so. The reporters, who originally treated the Bonnybridge phenomenon with seriousness, now wrote articles with amusing headlines that called Buchanan, and all the witnesses to the strangeness, into question. This opened the floodgates to a barrage of ridiculous UFO accounts sent in by every prankster in the country. By the 5th call, reporters and ufologists started to doubt that Zalus was *really* from Uranus at all.

After the Zalus town meeting, every single UFO encounter in Bonnybridge was discounted before any real research could be done. The whole phenomenon was considered a hoax from the start, and the abandoned research could have, who knows, got the world one step closer to finding evidence of life on other planets and visitors from other worlds.

Thanks, Zalus!

Here Come The Men in Black

Many people blamed Buchanan for the change in attitude towards the Bonnybridge sightings, claiming he cared more about milking the UFO stories for tourism than having any actual investigation done. But, was this the case?

There's no denying that Buchanan certainly had tourism on his mind. He had pitched the idea of having Bonnybridge twinned with Roswell, New Mexico for obvious reasons. He also had the idea of having a UFO visitor centre built in town. This was planned to be made of glass and shaped like a giant mushroom. This project, shockingly, never got off the ground. When a Japanese film crew turned up in town to do a report on the UFO flap, he expressed hope that it might result in a Mitsubishi factory being built in Bonnybridge.

Despite this, though, he did seem like a true believer in the UFO phenomena. He believed that Bonnybridge was a 'window area', a rip in the veil to whatever dimension aliens inhabited, which the extraterrestrials travelled through. He also claimed he had seen a UFO himself and was actively pushing the government to research strange encounters and unexplained sightings in the sky; something the government may not have liked.

Although no one else ever saw Zalus' messenger, Buchanan did describe him. He described him as being male, tall, thin, ageless, and wearing a black suit. A perfect description of one of the Men in Black.

No, not Will Smith or Tommy Lee Jones. The *actual* Men in Black are something far more sinister than Hollywood blockbuster fodder.

The MIB are supposedly a shadowy government agency tasked with keeping the UFO phenomena under wraps by any means necessary. Is it possible that the MIB sent an agent to feed the believing and, perhaps, slightly gullible Buchanan a ridiculous story about an extraterrestrial ambassador and an intergalactic embassy? Did they know he would repeat it to the townsfolk and the media and they would take the phenomena a lot less seriously and it would discredit the entire case? It's certainly a tactic that has been reported in other MIB cases from around the globe.

The other possibility involves a different MIB theory. There are many people who believe that the Men in Black are not involved with any government. There are people who believe that the Men in Black are not even human. Theories range from the MIB being alien in origin themselves, and even extend to the MIB being demons, vampires, time travellers, and that's just for starters. What all these theories have in common is that Men in Black have their own agenda in regards to the UFO phenomenon.

Ever since the Men in Black rose to prominence in the world of the paranormal after harrassing the ufologist Albert Bender in the early 1950s, they have varied in appearance and displayed a variety of abilities.

Though the trademark black suit is a constant in all encounters, other visual elements of the MIB have been more unusual and subject to change. Those who have met one have described their skin as fake looking, almost like plastic pulled over a skeleton. Others have described their lips as looking painted on, and even smearing off after being rubbed. Others have said that they lack eyelids, eyebrows, and fingernails. Sometimes they wear gloves, hats, sunglasses, and as we'll see later, even weirder fashion choices such as helmets and goggles.

What remains the same in all these descriptions is the belief that the MIB are something not human attempting to *look* human. As for abilities, the MIB have been reported to be able to communicate with a person telepathically. They have been able to subject a person to something not unlike hypnotism. They have been able to teleport, appearing somewhere suddenly one second then vanishing the next. They have been able to disrupt and damage technology without ever being near it. They have the ability to destroy or vanish solid matter. All of these abilities have been used to harass, intimidate and silence witnesses, researchers and proponents of the UFO phenomenon.

Whoever or whatever this mysterious Man In Black was, he certainly succeeded in destroying the credibility of the Bonnybridge encounters, whether that was his/its intention or not. Some now believe that the MIB was just a case of mistaken identity, and the name Zalus came from an unrelated UFO report. Others believe that Buchanan never even mentioned the name Zalus, and the story was just put out there to discredit him and the case. Real or not though, Zalus was the final nail in the coffin for the Bonnybridge phenomenon.

Looking back on the Bonnybridge UFOs, especially the pre-Zalus sightings and encounters, many of the reports have a great degree of uniqueness and high strangeness, something that lends a lot of believability to them. Had these initial sightings been researched properly, perhaps some great breakthrough in ufology could have been made. Perhaps this is why the MIB decided to discredit Bonnybridge.

Or maybe Zalus was real and everyone ignored his important message. Oops.

Embrace The Weird

Although Buchanan caught some flak for possibly having tourism on the brain, is now the time for Bonnybridge to consider that maybe he had the right idea, just at the wrong time?

Towns across America that have had weird stories attached to them have capitalised on them in the years since. When Flatwoods in Braxton County was visited by a tall, humanoid, possibly-semi-robotic alien with glowing eyes, the locals were understandably shaken up for a bit. After some time had passed though, they decided "Why not take advantage?" A museum was opened dedicated to The Flatwoods Monster, some tourist sites (including giant chairs shaped like the monster) were placed around town, and now it's the main reason to go and visit.

In West Virginia, Point Pleasant has also taken full advantage of the time that the Mothman took up residency in the old TNT area just outside of town. Mothman appeared in 1966 and stayed until late 1967, and brought with him a whole manner of other weird stuff. During his time in Point Pleasant, locals also reported seeing UFOs, experiencing poltergeist activity, and receiving visits from the Men in Black. Sure, having a giant dark humanoid with a massive wingspan and red eyes was terrifying for locals at the time, but years later they also decided to take advantage. They opened a Mothman museum and even dedicated a whole festival to the cryptid. Every year, the town is flooded with tourists and paranormal fans.

Even in Scotland, Loch Ness has taken full advantage of the tourism Nessie can bring. They have boat tours, a museum, and an entire army's worth of cuddly toys to buy. Is it time for Bonnybridge to take its place as Scotland's UFO capital, and make a few quid while they're at it? Who wouldn't want to visit a UFO museum in town and buy a cuddly Zalus to take home? Maybe now is even the right time to get the giant glass mushroom off the ground.

Interestingly, Bonnybridge is itself in a paranormal hotspot known as The Falkirk Triangle. We'll be paying a few more visits to this area before we're finished.

The Grey Man

We've all heard of Bigfoot, Sasquatch, and the Yeti: large and hairy humanoid creatures said to exist in the heavily wooded areas of just about every continent on the globe.

While many believe these ape men exist, the scientific community is more sceptical. There is very little evidence to suggest their existence outside of the occasional foot print or hair sample, many of which go on to be proven to belong to an already known animal, or a total hoax. This lack of physical evidence but abundance of experiences and sightings have led to theories revolving around these cryptids being more than mere physical animals.

Some have suggested these creatures could, in fact, be more paranormal than anyone has given them credit for. Some think that these Bigfoots (Bigfeet?) could actually be spirits, appearing and disappearing at will. Although they can be seen and interact with humans, they leave no trace of their presence, explaining the lack of evidence towards their existence.

Others believe that these furry fiends are indeed physical creatures, but are not of this world. They believe that they travel to our world from their own through dimensional wormholes, and leave the same way before they have a chance to leave any evidence that would prove they are real. Whether they can control these wormholes, or whether they occur at random, is also a point of debate.

There are many different ideas and theories around what Bigfoot is, where it comes from, why its existence has never been proved, and what it would mean if it was. The answer, surprisingly, may be hidden in the Scottish Highlands.

The Bigfoot of Ben MacDhui

The Grey Man, or The Big Grey Man, or, in Gaelic/Klingon, Fear Liath Mor, is a creature or entity said to inhabit a mountain in the Cairngorms called Ben MacDhui, with encounters dating back to the 1700's.

Sightings are rare, but those who have encountered The Grey Man describe it as a yeti-like creature who is upwards of ten feet tall, with unusually long arms and legs, an ape's head, and covered in short hair or fur. Though sightings are rare, encounters are not. This is because most people who have a run in with The Grey Man never actually see it.

It is most often encountered by lone hikers high on the mountain when the mist rolls in. Those who encounter it, first report a feeling of being watched. They then hear the sound of footsteps following them, crunching in the snow. Then, finally, they see a huge shadow looming through the mist, coming straight for them. Usually, the person encountering the creature chooses to run away as quickly as possible at this point, so they never get a good proper gander at the beast. A fairly understandable reaction, I would say.

Sightings (Kind Of)

Although tales of the Grey Man on Ben MacDhui go back hundreds of years, the story that brought it to public attention came in 1925. The encounter actually took place in 1891, but it would not be revealed until more than 30 years later.

J. Norman Collie, a seasoned climber, had just reached the summit of Ben MacDhui as the mist began to roll in. As he started his descent, the mist grew thick and visibility fell. He began to feel uneasy, and heard footsteps following him with no discernible source. This alarmed Collie, as he had seen no one else on his ascent. What's more, he claimed that the footsteps sounded three or four times longer than his own strides, suggesting a leg length that a human couldn't possibly have, unless on stilts. Collie sped up, but the sound of the footsteps grew louder and closer to him. It seemed to Collie like he was in a high altitude version of *Silent Hill*.

Collie, a normally rational man, was suddenly gripped by fear and bravely fled down the remaining 5 miles of the mountain. When he reached the bottom, he vowed to never return alone.

Although Collie's story popularised The Grey Man, it was far from the first, or last, encounter.

Mountaineer Alexander Tewnion had his own experience on Ben MacDhui in October of 1943. He claimed that as he reached the peak of the mountain, mist enveloped the summit. The atmosphere became dark and oppressive, and footsteps started to echo from within the fog. Soon, Alexander spotted a large figure in the mist that seemed to be watching him. Then, suddenly, the figure charged at him. Alexander drew his standard issue mountaineer's revolver and fired three shots into the charging figure. Luckily, it wasn't a lost hiker, and did appear to be some terrifying paranormal creature (phew). It didn't even flinch at the bullets, let alone slow down.

Convinced his firearm and other conventional weapons would be of no use here, Alexander turned and fled down the mountain in what he says was a personal best time. Sometimes you just need the right motivation. Tewnion was in no doubt that he had encountered The Grey Man, and would maintain the existence of the entity for the rest of his life.

The Grey Man Explained?

The uneasy feelings, the footsteps, and the figure in the mist are usual in every Grey Man encounter, and something many people have tried to debunk.

The feeling of being watched that comes before the footsteps are heard has been put down to exhaustion and isolation. While this may explain these feelings in less experienced hikers, it seems unlikely in cases involving more experienced mountaineers. Alexander Tewnion was on a ten day solo hike, so he was hardly the type to be bothered by a bit of alone time.

Infrasound (sound below the level of human audibility) is another explanation that has been given for these feelings. These soundwaves can make the listener feel uneasy and anxious, while they are unaware they are even hearing them. Infrasound has been discovered in locations thought to be haunted, and has explained some of the sensations felt in these places. Could it also exist on Ben MacDhui?

The sound of footsteps has been explained away as being made by animals. There are certainly deer and wild cats on the mountain, but that doesn't explain the impossibly large size of the strides. Some people have claimed these have been caused by "double footfall". When a person steps on snow covered ground, it can take a few seconds for the snow to totally collapse. By the time it does, the person has already walked forward several paces and the collapsing could sound like someone following close behind. If this only happened on every third or fourth step, it would give the impression of giant strides.

The figure people have seen in the mist has been explained as a phenomenon with a name fit for a metal band: "Brocken Spectre" (named for where it was first discovered; Brocken, the highest peak of the Harz mountain range in Germany). This is a rare meteorological occurrence that takes place when the sun casts a person's shadow onto a wall of mist or fog. The result is that the person's shadow is projected onto the mist as a huge, imposing, humanoid, shadowy monster. If the person viewing it was unaware that they were looking at their own shadow, it could look to them like some oversized monster coming to get them.

As unbelievable as this Brocken Spectre phenomenon may sound, there is actually a famous case of it happening on Ben MacDhui. In 1791, the poet James Hogg was tending sheep on the mountain when he was suddenly confronted by a terrifying, 30 foot tall creature approaching him from inside a cloud of fog. Terrified, he ran home. Realising he had left his sheep behind, he built up the nerve to return the next day.

As he ascended, the mist rolled in and he was once again confronted by the giant creature. This time, though, he realised the creature was wearing a hat. A hat very similar to his own. And when James took his hat off, so did the creature. It was at this point that he realised he was literally afraid of his own shadow.

These explanations however do not account for those who claim to have actually seen The Grey Man, not just a figure in the mist.

In the early 1920's, the president of the Moray Mountaineering Club Tom Crowley (no relation) was descending the mountain when he glanced behind himself to check his route. By chance, he saw something terrifying approaching. He saw a tall grey figure, with long legs, and talons on its hands and feet. Understandably, and much like everyone else who encountered The Grey Man, he ran the rest of the way down.

Supernatural Explanations

While these explanations are all reasonable and rational, can they really explain away every single (non physical) encounter with The Grey Man? It seems unlikely that infrasound, double footfall, and Brocken Spectre could all occur one after the other, and so often.

This has led some to come up with less scientific explanations. Could The Grey Man be a ghost?

Some have theorised that The Grey Man could be the spirit of a hiker that died on the mountain, who now haunts lone mountaineers when they are near the summit, attempting to make them turn back and avoid a similar fate. An interesting theory, but there have been no reports of a hiker dying on Ben MacDhui before Grey Man encounters began. It also does not explain The Grey Man's size and monstrous appearance.

Could The Grey Man be a physical creature, one as of yet undiscovered by science, similar to a Yeti or Bigfoot? Could a cryptid, or family of cryptids, have been living, breeding, and surviving on Ben MacDhui? Or perhaps a single creature with an insanely long lifespan? The lack of physical evidence and its seemingly supernatural abilities, doesn't point towards it.

Could The Grey Man be something of a mix of two previous theories? The Grey Man has the appearance of a cryptid of some sort, but the abilities of a ghost or phantom. Could The Grey Man be the ghost of a Yeti? Could, in ancient times, a Yeti-like creature have lived on Ben MacDhui, died there, but its spirit remains? We have reports of ghost cats, ghost dogs, even ghost trains, is a ghost Yeti so unlikely?

Some Buddhists believe that Ben MacDhui is the home of a

Bodhisattva. A Bodhisattva is a perfected being who observes human life. Could The Grey Man be one? Its aggressiveness towards hikers certainly doesn't suggest it wants to merely observe life. Also, would a perfected being look like a hairy giant with gangly limbs?

One final theory (and a theory we will revisit several times in this book) is that The Grey Man is a tulpa or egregore.

Basically, a tulpa is a thoughtform energy ghost. A creature created through the sheer belief in it. Something that takes on a life of its own simply through the attention and latent psychic energy directed at it. Could these rational explanations and natural phenomena such as infrasound, double footfall, and Brocken Spectre have created the legend of The Grey Man, and then the collective belief and fear people have for this entity have simply willed it into physical existence?

If so there may indeed be a large, hairy humanoid creature lurking on Ben MacDhui, ready to attack anyone who dares climb its mountain.

While this may explain The Grey Man, its connections to the furry humanoids of North America and Tibet cannot be ignored.

Why are there so many reports of strange ape-like creatures across the world, and why can't their existence be proved? Are these creatures related? Are they physical creatures at all? Are they travelling here from another place, another dimension? If so, for what purpose? Perhaps if we could find physical evidence of The Grey Man, or evidence of where it comes from, we would be closer to closing the case on Bigfoot, Yeti, and Sasquatch.

The Glasgow Witches

Witches are usually associated with Salem, Massachusetts and for good reason. It's the site of the world's most famous witch trials. Hundreds of men and women were accused of the crime of practising witchcraft, thirty were found guilty, and nineteen were brutally executed. It became the unofficial home of witchcraft, with a huge tourism industry built around it. Nothing brings in the crowds quite like horrific murders.

Unknown to many though, Glasgow had its own witch trials; the events surrounding which were arguably far stranger than anything that happened in Salem.

A Mystery Illness & A Psychic

On the 14th of October 1676, Sir George Maxwell set out for a business meeting in the centre of Glasgow. Unfortunately, on his way there he was struck with a terrible illness. He lost all of his energy and collapsed, sweating profusely. Later, he recalled feeling as if he was being stabbed in his left side with a knife. Onlookers rushed to help him, and he assured them that he wasn't just having a whitey (a Scottish slang term for when you turn pale and sickly after smoking too much narcotics).

He was carried back to Pollock Hall, a huge estate that he owned, and doctors were summoned. Many came to try and diagnose Maxwell but none could determine what had inflicted him, or how to cure it. Luckily, Maxwell had someone else who could diagnose him, but it was no medical professional.

Not long before Maxwell's sudden sickness his daughters had become friends with a teenage girl named Janet Douglas, who worked on their estate.

Janet had arrived in Glasgow earlier that year from the Highlands and had quickly made a name for herself as a psychic. When she arrived in the city she was apparently a mute, but regained her ability to speak only to tell a local goldsmith that the cause for his failing business was a curse he had been victim to. Nothing, of course, to do with his poor customer service.

She claimed that a saboteur had made a clay model of him, carved his name into it, and hidden it inside the shop. Janet claimed this was part of an evil spell meant to drive customers away. The goldsmith was understandably sceptical of the claims this girl he'd never met was making, but decided to give his shop a thorough inspection anyway. Sure enough, hidden in his shop he found a small clay statuette with his name carved into it.

Visions & Witches

When Janet learned of her new friends' father's mystery illness, she offered up her own explanation. An explanation that had come to her in the form of a psychic vision.

In her vision Janet had seen Janet Mathie, a local woman, creating a male figurine out of wax and chanting, while sticking pins into it. She said that Mathie was trying to kill Maxwell through witchcraft. Maxwell, having exhausted other options and being an avid witch hunter himself, decided to humour Janet and sent her, along with two of his employees, to Mathie's house.

Somehow, either by breaking and entering or asking nicely, they got into Mathie's home. Janet went right to the fireplace and found a wax figure with pins pushed into it. When she revealed her discovery to George Maxwell, his son; John, had Mathie imprisoned. John believed absolutely that Mathie would try to curse his father. Mathie's son; Hugh, had worked for Maxwell until he was caught red-handed stealing. Maxwell fired the boy and threatened to have him arrested. Maxwell made this threat on October 14th, the very same day he was struck with the strange illness. A very unusual and damning coincidence.

Mathie protested her innocence, claiming that Janet had just made up her psychic vision and planted the wax figure in her fireplace to frame her. As there were already rumours that Mathie was involved in witchcraft, her protests fell on deaf ears. Her case wasn't helped by the fact that Maxwell made a miraculous recovery shortly after the wax figure was found.

As Mathie refused to confess she was left in prison to rot, the jailers believing she would eventually break down and admit to being in league with the devil, whether she actually was or not.

Soon after the new year, Maxwell was struck by his mystery illness once again.

With Mathie safely locked up, suspicion fell on her son; Hugh. Janet claimed she had yet another vision. In this one she saw Hugh making a new wax figure, pushing pins into it then hiding it under his bed. Hugh's cottage was searched and, predictably, the authorities found a wax figure under his bed. Like his mother, Hugh protested his innocence and swore Janet must have somehow broken in and placed it there. Despite his protests though, and just like his mother, he was arrested and placed in jail. While arresting Hugh, they also arrested his sister Annabelle, probably hoping to save themselves the bother of coming back later when Janet would inevitably have another vision.

Annabelle took a different approach from her mum and brother, and did not protest her innocence. She instantly admitted to not only her involvement in cursing Maxwell, but admitted to practising black magick and witchcraft, as well as to being in personal contact with Satan himself. Shortly after Hugh and Annabelle were arrested, Maxwell made another full recovery.

With the whole family in jail, they were each stripped and searched for a "Devil's Mark". This was a marking said to have been placed on a witches skin by Satan to signify their loyalty to the Dark Lord. In reality, the marks were usually nothing more than totally natural birthmarks, blemishes, moles or pimples. Unshockingly with the level of skincare found in the 1600's, Devil's Marks were found on all suspected witches.

Not long after the two new arrests, Janet had *another* vision.

In this vision she saw Mathie in her jail cell, fashioning yet another wax figure. Janet saw Mathie unable to find anything sharp to stab into the figurine, so she hid it under her bunk, possibly hoping she could carve a prison shiv later. Janet told the jailers, who promptly searched Mathie's cell.

They found another wax figurine under her bunk. Mathie once again claimed that it must have been planted there by Janet, but unlike her fireplace, no one could figure out how Janet could have possibly got into her cell and planted this figurine. Either way, the evidence towards Mathie and her family being evil witches was mounting.

The Trial

The trial against the Mathie family began on 27th January 1677.

After much mental and physical torture, it was "*discovered*" that the witches coven that had cursed Maxwell had been around for 40 years. The founding member, Margaret Jackson, had met the Devil while she was walking in Eastwood. Jackson was also arrested, and said that after a short but riveting conversation with the Devil, she agreed to be his servant in exchange for learning the secrets of dark magick. Soon after making her unholy pact with the Devil she recruited Mathie into her coven, along with a woman named Bessie Weir, and several others.

When Annabelle, the only Mathie to not initially deny any devil worship, took the stand, she doubled down on her story. Annabelle claimed that the Devil frequently visited her family in their cottage. She said he would appear as a man dressed all in black, with cloven hooves for feet. This goat man would usually get it on with Annabelle, leaving many to wonder where his goat half ended and his human half began.

During the family's time on the stand they claimed that after the first wax figure attack on Maxwell failed, Bessie Weir turned up at their cottage. They said that Weir told them that "The Master" wanted them to make a new wax figure to continue the curse on Maxwell. This was the figure that was found under the bed.

They admitted that revenge was the motivation behind the evil spells, and revenge was what the Devil had promised them.

As more members of the coven were named and arrested, some protested their innocence and others admitted their guilt. Either way, all were burned alive for their supposed crimes.

The only witch who escaped the death penalty was Annabelle. Strange, as she was the most outspoken about her guilt. Maybe her goat-legged lover worked some of his magick and got her a pardon. She spent some time in jail, before being transferred to a convent to be reformed.

John Maxwell also died not too long afterwards. Perhaps the witches continued their supernatural attacks from beyond the grave, or maybe the reformation of Annabelle Mathie wasn't too successful and she continued the curse.

What Happened to The Psychic?

Janet, whose supernatural powers were responsible for putting these women to their deaths, ended up in jail herself.

After the Mathie witch trials, the Maxwell family cut contact with Janet, perhaps worried that her visions would lead to her being accused of witchcraft and, by association, themselves. Janet continued to have her trademark visions, but this time she accused more prominent and successful people of being witches. This didn't have quite the same effect as accusing a poor, lower class family. Janet was arrested and jailed in Edinburgh, as the local authorities worried that her visions and accusations could lead to riots and violence.

During her time in prison she granted an interview to the author George Hickes. After their interview, Hickes was totally convinced that Janet had supernatural abilities. The only parts of her story that he doubted was that she was ever actually mute, and that she was actually from the Highlands. According to Hickes, she spoke too well for either to be true. Sorry, Highlanders.

Hickes believed that Janet was maybe the illegitimate child of someone in high society. A theory that gained credibility when Janet was suddenly and unexpectedly freed from jail.

Janet getting bailed out by an anonymous father or mother from high society, being brought home, and keeping a low profile for the rest of her life is the most generally accepted explanation behind her freedom and disappearance, but there are other theories.

One theory suggests she was banished from the country, possibly to Australia. Another theory suggests that the government at the time (and maybe even to this day) is run by a coven of witches who secretly control the country. It is suggested that they freed Janet and murdered her for bringing attention to the dark arts and having other witches killed. This theory is backed up by the fact that Annabelle was spared the death sentence, possibly suggesting she was involved with this higher society of witches.

One interesting theory states that she moved to the United States after she was freed and was somehow involved in the world famous Salem Witch Trials. As amazing as it would be to have this same girl involved in two very real and very deadly witch trails on two different continents, twenty years apart, would be; there is little to no evidence to suggest she was ever actually there.

A further theory suggests that Janet was freed so her powers could be used for good. Perhaps she was recruited by a kind of 1600's X-Men who wished to use her visions to hunt down and battle evil witches. This is the least likely theory, but definitely the most worthy of a cinematic adaptation.

Whether Janet was a psychic who had visions of the wrongdoings of witches, or if Annabelle got it on with a Satanic goatman, there is no denying it was a series of bizarre events and a court case for the ages.

Salem will always be the first thing that comes to mind when witch trials are mentioned, but perhaps Glasgow deserves a bit of recognition too, like an underrated B-side to a classic album.

The Wizard of Yester

Wizard.

   The word brings to mind old men with long grey beards wearing pointy hats and the unmistakable voice of Sir Ian McKellen telling you that *"you shall not pass!"*. While few people these days refer to themselves, or become known as, a wizard (terms like sorcerer, warlock, necromancer, and lich are far cooler) there was a time when it was the go-to label for anyone involved in anything remotely mystical.

   Most of these old-school wizards were likely just normal men and women interested in spirituality outside of the socially accepted religion of the time, but a few individuals really earned the title of wizard. These people had a reputation for casting spells, creating magical elixirs, entering into pacts with godlike beings, and summoning supernatural minions to do their bidding. One of these people who truly deserved the wizard title was a Scottish nobleman.

A Castle & A Wizard

Sir Hugo de Giffard, better known as The Wizard of Yester, was born in 1225 and was the son of an influential Scottish baron.

   Sir Hugo, prior to being known as The Wizard, was one of the guardians of Alexander III of Scotland and one of the regents of the kingdom. Giffard's father was given the land of Yesterd (as it was known before it was called Yester) by King William the Lion, and it was eventually passed down to Sir Hugo. It was on this land that Hugo decided to build a castle, and it was in this castle and during its construction, that he truly earned the name The Wizard of Yester.

When exactly construction began on Yester Castle is unknown, but it is known that it was completed before 1267. Who, or what, constructed the castle is up for debate.

In the undercroft, in the caverns below (a remnant of a previously constructed castle, by then long destroyed), it is said that Sir Hugo practised dark magick and even entered into a pact with the Devil. As a result of this satanic pact, Hugo was granted the ability to summon an army of hobgoblins which he used as slaves to build his castle.

Some say this is why certain rooms, tunnels and corridors in the castle seem to have been made to strange specifications. Many parts of the castle seem too small, with ceilings too low for humans to use or build. Believers of The Wizard and his hobgoblin army say this points towards the castle having been built by creatures that are smaller in size and stature than normal men. Perhaps greener in hue, too.

According to legend, no tools were heard during its construction, and it was built in record time. Some say that it was built in just one night, after the hobgoblins were summoned. They *are* an industrious race.

The subterranean hall where The Wizard made his unholy pact, known as Hobgoblin Hall (or Hobgoblin Ha'), is one of the few parts of the castle that has remained mostly intact to this day. A true testament to its builders' workmanship (be they human, hobgoblin, or otherwise).

Those who descend the narrow stairway down to this hall still report a sinister and haunting presence in the Ha', perhaps leftover dark magick from the wizards' occult rituals. From the hall, another corridor and staircase lead to what was thought to have once been a well. This area was blocked off by locals long ago, as they believed this well functioned as a gateway to hell. Perhaps this is where the hobgoblins marched up from this hell well when summoned.

The Cursed Pear

Sir Hugo's reputation as an evil wizard grew some years later when his daughter, Margaret, was to marry a member of the Clan Broun.

Hugo, perhaps not pleased with her choice of husband, gave him a pear he had picked himself. It seemed like a thoughtful, if unimpressive, wedding gift until Hugo revealed that he had cast a spell on this pear. He told his soon to be son-in-law that if anything should happen to this pear, his clan and family would be destroyed. The family obviously took this very seriously and encased the pear in a silver box. The pear stayed in this box for several hundred years, until it was unlocked in 1692 by a member of the Broun clan on her wedding night.

Why she decided to disturb the pear is unknown, but reportedly the fruit looked as fresh as it had when it was newly picked. The woman could not resist and took a bite. As soon as the bite was taken, the pear turned hard as a rock and misfortune suddenly plagued the family. Debts were amassed, properties were sold, members of the family were even killed in a flash flood. In 1718, without a male heir, the family line ended and the curse of the evil pear was complete.

As a result, Sir Hugo's reputation as a powerful wizard only grew, despite him having been dead for a few hundred years by this point.

The Hobgoblins Remain

Due to it being involved in multiple battles and sieges over the ages, much of Yester Castle is either destroyed or simply a shadow of its former self, but those who visit still describe a strange and otherworldly feeling in the air.

Approaching the castle now feels like something out of a medieval fantasy film. Many people have reported voices coming from within the woods with no known source. They have said that these noises are caused by the hobgoblins who still dwell in the area, hiding from humans. The woodland surrounding the castle makes the structure practically invisible until you're next to it; you can definitely picture a hobgoblin running around this area. And in 1972 that is exactly what Agnes McGaw saw.

Agnes was at an archaeological picnic on the grounds of Yester

Castle. Agnes and a friend were sitting on a fallen log, listening to a lecture about the castle and Sir Hugo. Agnes and her pal suddenly noticed an unusual "wee man" across from them, behind the lecturer. The strange man seemed to be silently mocking the lecturer. When the lecturer got to the legend of the hobgoblin's involvement, both women were sure this is what they were looking at.

The strange wee man quickly left the lecture, disappearing into the castle, and wasn't seen again. Agnes was left sure she had seen one of the castle builders.

Whether or not Sir Hugo had actual magical powers, conversed with the devil, cursed a pear, or summoned an army of industrious hobgoblins, there is no denying that this strange and mysterious character has left a lasting effect on Yester Castle and its legacy.

A75: The Ghost Road

We've all been told the stories and legends of haunted roads. I don't think there's anyone reading this book who, as a child or teenager, won't have heard the story of the phantom hitchhiker.

The story generally goes like this: a lone traveller drives down a long, dark and lonely road when they see someone by the side of it with their thumb out. Being a kind soul, they stop and give this hitchhiker a lift. As they drive, the passenger doesn't say much apart from their destination. Then the driver realises they are dressed strangely... as if from a different time.

When they arrive at the hitchhiker's destination, the lone traveller looks to their passenger side only to realise their passenger has vanished into thin air. The driver walks to the house, knocks on the door and is informed by a relative that they have been driving the ghost of their son, daughter, father, or some other family member who has been trying to get home since dying decades ago. And that this isn't the first time they've tried to catch a ride home.

It's a classic ghost story, and apart from the fright at the end and keeping generations of kids awake at night, it's relatively harmless. But some haunted roads are more sinister. Sometimes the spirits that haunt these roads don't just want to bum a ride. Sometimes it seems that these roads, and the phantoms that line them, are out to hurt drivers, throwing them into terrifying situations and even attempting to cause crashes.

The Ghost Road Strikes

A four mile long stretch on the A75, called the Kinmount Straight, is said to be the most haunted road in Scotland, and possibly even in the entire world. This reputation has earned it the spooky nickname of The Ghost Road.

A wide variety of apparitions have been described on this road over the years, some even being reported to the police. The ghostly figures seen on this road aren't limited to humanoid spectres though; they go as far as animals, unknown cryptid-like creatures, and even other vehicles.

The most famous case of the paranormal on the A75 occurred in 1962. Around midnight Derek and Norman Ferguson were driving along The Ghost Road. It was an easy, standard trip for them and they expected nothing out of the ordinary to occur on the empty road that night. That was until a hen flew straight towards their windscreen. The men braced for the impact this large bird would cause, but no impact came. It seemed that the hen vanished into thin air right before it collided with the glass. The men were confused, but assumed the hen had simply flown over their vehicle, as unlikely as that seemed. But phantom poultry wasn't all The Ghost Road had in store for them that night.

After the hen pulled its feathery disappearing act, an elderly woman ran towards the car waving her arms wildly, as if in some sort of distress. She seemed to come out of nowhere and gave the men no time to break. A collision of metal on flesh was certain. Much like the aforementioned hen, she disappeared into thin air just before being hit.

The men were now beginning to suspect that something was amiss on the A75. As if the men needed further proof that they were experiencing something outside the realms of the norm, they then reported that just after the old woman vanished, a man appeared in the road. This man was of an indeterminable age, had long wild hair, and was screaming incoherently. Once more, he vanished as soon as the car got close to him. Much like the hen and the woman, no impact or collision was heard or felt and the men were certain they hadn't hit anything or anyone with their car.

The Fergusons decided to get off this stretch of road as quickly as they could, and drove on without stopping to check if the man or woman were somehow still on the road or injured.

As they drove on, The Ghost Road decided to throw everything it had at them. It was as if the road didn't want them to leave. Or at least, it didn't want them to leave unharmed.

The men saw more animals on the road that vanished when they got near. They described seeing goats, dogs, even *more* hens, giant cats that looked like pumas, and creatures that they struggled to describe. The men drove on, ignoring this petting zoo of apparitions that emerged from the darkness and disappeared before their eyes.

After the menagerie of phantom animals, the temperature in the car dropped drastically. This was when the brothers decided to pull the car over. Perhaps they intended to see if the temperature was warmer outside, to see if there had been any damage done to the car, or maybe just to steady their nerves before continuing.

They parked by the side of the A75 and the car began to sway from side to side. It was as if there were people on either side, rocking it back and forth, all while high-pitched laughing could be heard. Derek leaped out of the car, either out of fear or in an attempt to catch the culprits. As soon as Derek had gotten out of the car, the unexplained movement stopped and the night was deathly quiet. Derek looked around, there was nowhere anyone could have escaped to in such a short span of time. He got back in, and they decided to keep driving. This was when The Ghost Road pulled out the big guns.

For the first time in their journey along the A75, Derek and Norman saw another vehicle. A furniture van was driving towards them from the opposite direction. The brothers felt some relief to finally see someone else on the road after all this weirdness. The relief was to be short lived though. The furniture van was coming right for them, speeding towards their car in a direct collision course. The men braced, but nothing happened. Much like the hen this all started with, the furniture van disappeared just before it crashed into their car.

The Ferguson brothers' terrifying car ride has become paranormal legend and is the best known story of The Ghost Road, but is far from the only story or encounter that had taken place here.

Peasants & Sackheads

Bob Sturgeon used to operate a snack van on the side of the A75 and became used to hearing ghostly stories from truck drivers when they stopped for a coffee and a bite. The stories were so common and frequent that Sturgeon estimated he would hear around one a week. He said that although these encounters were all individual experiences from people who had never met each other, there were some recurring themes.

Sturgeon reported that a lot of the truck drivers who confided in him described the apparitions they saw as looking out of the medieval age. Specifically, they looked like downtrodden medieval peasants. One truck driver, after telling Sturgeon his story, was so traumatised that he quit his driving job altogether.

This terrified driver told Bob that he had been parked in a layby on the Kinmount Straight, sleeping in his truck for the night. He was woken up at around 3 in the morning, seemingly without reason. When he looked out of his window, he saw what he described as a parade of people walking along the road. They were dressed in an out of time fashion and, according to the driver, seemed to go on forever. He was so shocked and terrified by this sight that he froze in his truck, unable to move until this bizarre medieval ghost parade had finally passed and vanished.

Truck drivers aren't the only people outside of The Ferguson Brothers to have strange experiences on this road.

In March 1995, a married couple were driving along The Ghost Road, unaware of its reputation, when they saw a man with a sack on his head approaching the car with his arms stretched out to meet them. They hit this man at 60 mph, but heard no sound nor felt an impact. They screeched to a stop and got out of their car. They found no body. They were so concerned that they contacted the police and reported what had happened. The authorities could find no logical explanation.

A similar incident occurred in July 1997. A mother was driving with her two children along the road. As she drove, a man leaped out in front of her car. The woman braked hard, trying to save the man from the impact of the car, but it was too late - or so the woman thought. There was no sound of impact. There was no body on the road. The woman was so sure she had hit and possibly killed this man that she also contacted the police and reported what had happened. Once again, they could find no explanation.

What Controls The Ghost Road?

Why is the A75 such a hotspot for the paranormal? Could something have happened on this land hundreds of years ago, before the road was built? The spirits of those who died here now doomed to haunt this stretch of road for eternity? If this is the case, then why do animals and vehicles appear here?

While the ghosts of animals are far from a new concept, an entire barnyard seems strange. And what about the big cats? And the animals that could not be described; like cryptids? And of course, what about the phantom furniture truck? Perhaps the memory of a truck that crashed on the road many years ago?

Or could the road be controlled by a malevolent entity? A power outside of space and time that gets its kicks by throwing bizarre psychic projections at drivers that dare to traverse its domain in an attempt to make them crash? Could the A75 not be haunted by a laundry list of various ghosts, but by one strange entity that has slipped through the veil and now resides on this road, unable (or unwilling) to show itself, but able to affect the fabric of reality on this small stretch now known as The Ghost Road?

The Blairgowrie
UFOs

Crop circles are a strange phenomena that are often found in the same rural areas and timeframe as UFO sightings. Although these circles rose to popularity and common knowledge in the 1970's, there have been reports of them from as far back as the 1600's and beyond.

A crop circle is believed to be an indent made by the landing of an extraterrestrial craft. Often these extraterrestrial indents are (as the name suggests) simple circles, suggesting the landing of something like a flying saucer. Over the years though, more unusual and exotically shaped crop circles have also been found. Some have been a series of circles in different sizes. Some have been complex geometric patterns. Some have even looked like an abstract and indecipherable code, leading some to believe that crop circles may be more than simple landing spots, but an attempt at communication from beyond.

Finding a crop circle is usually the conclusion of an alien experience. Finding some sort of physical evidence of visitors from another world puts a nice little full stop at the end of the tale (and lends it some credibility). Sometimes though, the discovery of a crop circle is just the beginning of the story.

Circles Appear

In June of 1990 Scotland's first crop circles appeared in a field on the edge of the town of Blairgowrie. This attracted the attention of UFO investigators Ron Halliday and Ken Higgins.

In their investigation in and around Blairgowrie they discovered that unexplained balls of light had been seen several times in an area close to where the crop circles had appeared. The circles themselves were seventy feet across, and while investigating them Halliday and Higgins could find no evidence of them being man made. What's more, no one has ever stepped forward to claim responsibility for creating them, like in other crop circle pranks. They also weren't shaped like anything phallic, a sure sign that no human tricksters were involved. This gave these circles a large amount of credibility.

This credibility kept the two investigators in town, and they soon discovered that the strange lights were far from the first UFO sightings in Blairgowrie. The pair discovered that in the 18th century a large ball of flame was described flying above the River Ericht. It travelled several miles along the banks and left destruction in its wake, even blowing up houses on its journey. Many claimed this could only have been a UFO, though it would be a rare case of a UFO behaving violently. Perhaps the pilot was still getting the hang of the controls.

The Yale Key UFO

More recently, Halliday and Higgins discovered that a single family had several strange experiences in 1984 - 6 years before the crop circles appeared.

On April 25th at 5:30pm Mrs. Gwen Freeman was sitting in her back garden weaving a tapestry, something that would have been more at home back in the 18th century. As she weaved, she noticed the family dog looking scared. Just as the dog ran back inside, Gwen claimed she was enveloped by a cloud of light. It lasted only seconds and she was temporarily blinded, but no permanent damage was done.

When the light cloud released her and her sight returned she saw a bush five feet in front of her glowing and sparkling. As she stared at the shiny bush she realised it was being hit by a beam of light from above. As she followed the beam skywards, she was shocked to see it was coming from a large silver object that she described as bulbous and with a long tail. As she watched the object, lights around the front of the craft began to turn on, and the beam of light stopped.

Gwen shouted for her son, Sid Jr., who was doing some weeding in the front garden. He hurried to see what his mother wanted, but by the time he got to the back garden and looked where Gwen was pointing, the object had drastically decreased in size, as if moving away at a high speed, without leaving any sort of trail in the sky or making any sound. There was a bright flash, and the object was gone. As they looked back in the garden, the bush had also returned to its normal non-glowing self.

Gwen, Sid Jr., and Sid Sr. didn't know what to do after spotting this strange object, so they phoned the local police. Two officers rushed to the scene shortly after, listened to Gwen's story, and inspected the garden.

As they scoured the garden for clues, the family overheard the officers talking and got some information they were not meant to. They heard the officers talk about how a similar object had been reported elsewhere in Blairgowrie, those witnesses describing the object as looking like a giant Yale key. A description that matched Gwens. The officers took some soil samples and leaves from the once glowing bush and left. The Freeman family never heard from the officers, or the police, ever again.

When the UFO investigators went to the police station in 1990 to ask whether anything had been discovered from the samples taken, they were met with confusion. Despite still having many of the same employees and officers in the station as were there in 1984, no one could remember such an unusual incident being reported and none could remember investigating it.

After being asked to wait for quite some time, the investigators got a very unsatisfactory answer. They were told the report was likely transferred to another station and/or destroyed. In other words: they had no idea who had investigated it, who took the samples, who made the report, or what happened to it. The impression given was that the police had nothing to do with it, and perhaps another organisation had taken charge.

Back in 1984, a few days after Gwen's UFO sighting, the Freeman family heard a rumbling sound coming from outside. They ran to their backdoor and into the garden, and were surprised to see a military helicopter hovering above their house. Beneath the helicopter two boxlike devices were hanging; one black and one orange. The family got the feeling that the helicopter was using these devices to film the area and test the air.

Sid Jr. phoned the nearest RAF station to try and get some answers. After some amount of time waiting on the line he was told that the helicopter was simply out on manoeuvres and not to worry. Two days later, the helicopter appeared again and seemed to be repeating the same tests with the box devices. It did not return for a third time. The RAF had never done manoeuvres like this in Blairgowrie before or since.

The Impolite MIB

As Halliday and Higgins continued investigating Blairgowrie and the Freeman family, they asked Gwen if anything else strange had happened on April 25th; the day she saw the key-shaped craft. She remembered that at around midday, mere hours before she saw the UFO, she saw twelve men, all dressed in black suits, walking down her street in single file. Sound familiar? This isn't the last time we'll be meeting the Men in Black.

The twelve men walked up to a neighbour's house and entered it without so much as knocking. The MIB are not known for their good manners. Worried, Gwen went to the neighbours house to make sure everything was alright. She went over and knocked on the door. The neighbour answered, and Gwen explained what she had seen. The neighbour was confused. He explained that there was no one else in the house, and that the door was locked.

The MIB appearing after a UFO sighting is common, but before one is rarer. It's hard to imagine that they weren't somehow connected to the sighting of the strange object in the sky. But how were they connected? They arrived first, so was the UFO following them for some reason? Perhaps in pursuit of them, like an intergalactic police force? Or were the MIB there first to try and protect the town from the UFO and its inhabitants? Perhaps they feared another fireball incident. The connection between aliens, UFOs and the MIB is the subject of much debate, but if we can figure out why they appeared in Blairgowrie before the UFO sighting we may be closer to our answer.

And is there any connection between the crop circles that brought the investigators to Blairgowrie in the first place, the UFO and MIB sightings 6 years earlier, and perhaps even the ball of flame from the 18th century?

Could the ship from all three sightings be the same, albeit on fire in one incident? Could this ship have made the crop circles, with locals only able to see its glowing light at night? Were the MIB here to attack the UFO? Study it? Research it? Or was the MIB the crew of this UFO?

Many have theorised that the Men in Black are in fact extraterrestrial beings themselves (along with ultra and intraterrestrials), could their connection to this UFO sighting, and many other sightings across the globe, be far more personal than we think?

The Freeman family never described the officers who came to investigate their garden, but I would not be surprised if they mentioned that they were wearing black suits.

The Trouble at Ringcroft

What is a poltergeist?

A poltergeist is a particularly angry spirit. While a common ghost is content to quietly appear and walk through walls, a poltergeist is more likely to smash plates, steal and hide objects, rip the bedsheets off you in the night, and even physically attack a living person. While poltergeists are rarer than a casual haunting, for those who experience it, it is a far more terrifying and life changing ordeal.

Poltergeist Problems

In 1695, a farm called (*deep breath*) The Ringcroft of Stocking, in the Parish of Rerrick, in the town of Auchencairn, in the region of Dumfries and Galloway encountered one of the strangest and most severe cases of poltergeist activity ever reported in Scotland.

The farm was owned by Andrew Mackie and his family, and the first incident took place in February of that year. Andrew discovered one morning that his cattle had all managed to break free of their tethers during the night. He thought it was strange that all his cattle would be able to do this all at the same time, but assumed it was an issue with either the strength of the tether, or how tightly it was tied. Annoyed, Andrew gathered up his cattle from around the farm. The following night he used stronger tethers and tied them as tightly as he could.

The next morning though, the same thing had happened. Every one of his cattle had escaped again. He then moved his animals to another outbuilding, perhaps thinking it was somehow the fault of where he was keeping them. The next day, he found one of the cows had been moved from the outbuilding and was tied to the farmhouse itself. It was tied in such a way that it was suspended in the air, its feet barely touching the ground. It was left hanging, mooing in confusion. Whoever tied it like this would have to have had considerable strength to lift an adult cow.

Soon after the strange incidents of the escape artist cattle, something weirder and far more dangerous occurred.

Late at night, while all the family were asleep, someone made a large pile of peat on the floor in the centre of the house. As if making this stinking pile of decomposing vegetable matter in the house wasn't enough for whatever was tormenting the Mackie family, it then set it on fire.

Luckily the smoke woke the family and they were able to put the fire out before anyone was hurt or any serious damage was done. No peat piling culprit could be found, despite how hard the family searched their home and farm.

Things Get Worse

In March, things got violent again. Something began launching volleys of stones both at the house from outside, and at the family inside. They could not find where the stones were being thrown from, or what was throwing them. The stone throwing was worst on Sundays, and was aimed mostly at those in prayer. This seemed intentional, as if whoever or *whatever* was attacking the family was not a fan of Christianity.

In April, some of the Mackie children entered the living room and saw an odd humanoid figure covered in a blanket, sitting by the fire. They were obviously scared, given the recent unexplainable events in and around their home, but tried to talk to the figure to get its attention. The figure sat perfectly still and ignored them. One of the children eventually worked up the courage to walk over to the figure, and discovered it was simply a stool that had been turned upside down with a blanket carefully placed over it, as if intentionally to look like a human figure. There was no one in the house at this time who could have done this.

A Curse

As the stone attacks got worse and worse towards those trying to pray, Andrew Mackie decided to contact the local minister: Mr. Telfer.

Telfer arrived on the farm a couple of days later, and he and Mackie discussed what could be causing these strange paranormal events. Telfer told Mackie that years before he and his family lived on the farm, it was owned by a family called McNaught. The McNaught father had constant bad luck on the farm, such as poor crops and a variety of health problems that only happened after he moved in. McNaught had started to believe the farm was cursed.

McNaught sent his son to see a local woman who was known to be a psychic, thinking she could help. The son found her and got her expert advice. She told him that the farm was indeed cursed, and the way to break it was simple. At the entrance of the house there was a stone slab. She told him to find the tooth hidden beneath it and burn it, or the curse would continue.

He rushed home to tell his father, but on his way ran into a recruitment party. He was enlisted into the army there and then, probably without his consent. The son was sent to war, where he met another man, John Redick, who just so happened to be from the same Parish as he was, and who was about to go home on leave. The son asked John to pass on the psychic's message to his father when he arrived home. John agreed.

When John arrived at the farm ready to pass on McNaught Jr.'s message from the psychic, he realised he had arrived too late. McNaught had died, possibly as a result of the curse.

John decided not to bother telling the new owner about the curse (that wasn't part of the deal after all), and instead went to the local minister. Not to call the minister loose-lipped, but word did get around and the new owner did move the stone slab, and did find a tooth under it. He burned it, as instructed, and never experienced anything strange on the farm. This story had been passed on to Telfer (the minister now dealing with the poltergeist) by the minister who spoke to Redick, and he had no reason to doubt it.

Priest Versus Poltergeist

With a curse seeming likely, Telfer and Mackie got to work.

Telfer walked around the farm, ready to spring into action and do battle with the first unholy spirit he saw, but he experienced nothing out of the ordinary. As he was gearing up to leave though, a stone flew over his head and at the house. The family quickly declared it to be the work of the poltergeist who had been tormenting them. The minister agreed to return on the Sunday and lead the family in prayer in hopes of driving this evil spirit out.

That Sunday, when Telfer and the family were at prayer, they were all again pelted by pebbles with no attacker in sight. Now convinced that the family was indeed under attack from a malevolent entity, Telfer agreed to return in *another* couple of days, better prepared, to stay the night to try and vanquish the evil force.

A few days passed, and Telfer returned ready to do battle. Telfer started by leading another prayer, because that worked so well the last time. Predictably, he had stones launched at him again. This time though, the spirit decided to take it up a notch.

The family heard a loud crack and saw Telfer doubled over in pain. He claimed he felt as if he had been whacked on the back by a large, heavy staff or plank of wood. There was no such weapon to be seen. He recomposed himself only to be hit again and again by the same invisible weapon. The Mackie family all continued to hear the sound of it colliding with his skin.

As Telfer powered through, continuing the prayers, knocks and bangs were heard around the room, with no obvious source. Those in attendance said the noises sounded like someone or something trying to find an entryway into the house through the walls.

The minister, still attempting to pray, then felt something pressing on his arm. When he looked down, he saw a pure white hand gripping him. The hand was connected to an arm that ran up to an elbow, which connected to a… nothing. What seemed to be grabbing him, levitating in the air, was a pale and disembodied arm, in a scene that must have looked like the cover of *The Slip* by Nine Inch Nails. It appeared Telfer had failed in combating the spirit

In the coming days, the spirit continued its violent spree. Neighbours who tried to visit the Mackies were driven away from the house by a bombardment of stones being thrown at them and the feeling of being whacked by a large, unseen staff. Inside the house, the spirit continued to torment the family.

Mackies were dragged around the house by an invisible presence. When they tried to sleep, their blankets were ripped off of them and they were pulled out of bed. Furniture was moved when no one was looking, chests and wardrobes violently shook and of course, the hail of stones continued.

Telfer, still keen to vanquish the evil, decided to put a team together. He called on some more ministers to help him fight what was now being known as "The Trouble".

When they arrived at the house, The Trouble wasted no time getting to work. Rocks, much larger than before, were lobbed at them as they entered. One of the ministers suffered a bloody head wound from a stone hit and then, to add insult to injury, had his wig ripped off. More peat appeared and spontaneously caught fire, which was then also lobbed at the visiting ministers. Even the combined might of these ministers, these holy Avengers, could not stop The Trouble.

A Curse Lifted?

It seemed that the Mackies were out of options and no one could save them. This was when Mrs. Mackie realised there was a loose slab by the front door. She lifted it and underneath found seven small bones, flesh, and some dry blood all contained in an old, folded piece of paper.

She gathered up these items and brought them to Telfer. While she removed them, The Trouble attacked again. Stones were thrown, fireballs landed in the house, and bedsheets burst into flame. After the strange items were in the minister's possession though, the attack stopped dead.

In the middle of April, the Mackie family briefly moved out and had some neighbours watch the house. Perhaps they felt like they were due a little holiday, or possibly they wanted some guinea pigs to see if the removal of the items under the slab had banished The Trouble, or just pissed it off even more.

The neighbours reported no strange activity so the Mackies moved back in, thinking the curse was broken now that the items were in the possession of Telfer.. Almost as soon as they returned, so did The Trouble. Now, The Trouble seemed to be growing in confidence, even finding its voice. When it struck someone, the invisible entity could be heard to say "Take you that!". The stone throwing and pyromania also returned in earnest, along with a bit of literal mudslinging thrown in.

A few days after moving back in, The Trouble began to speak to Mr. Mackie. It told him he would be tormented for another four days. Mackie asked the spirit where it came from, and it told him that God had sent it to warn the land to repent. It also told Mackie that if he prayed and worshipped it instead of God, then the torment would stop. Mackie recognised this as the voice of the Devil, and refused.

The End of The Trouble

The next day, the house caught fire.

The Mackie family and neighbours fought all day to put it out, but despite their best efforts the building was mostly destroyed by the pyromaniac poltergeist. A few days later members of the community met in the cowshed, where this all began, and took part in a group prayer to try and get rid of The Trouble once and for all. As they prayed, they saw a black mass in a corner that grew like a dark cloud until it filled the whole room. Those praying had mud flung at them, and some felt like they were being violently grabbed with such force it would leave marks and bruises.

Suddenly, after much prayer, the dark cloud disappeared and The Trouble was gone. On its way out it set fire to a sheep shed, but this was its last act of terror.

It seemed they had got rid of The Trouble too late however, as the farmhouse (and a sheep shed) had already burned to the ground. They could not afford to have it rebuilt and so the Mackie family soon moved on. Today, all that remains on the site of The Ringcroft Farm is a dead tree.

Telfer later wrote the entire story of the happenings at Ringcroft in a pamphlet called "A True Relation of an Apparition, Expressions and Actings of a Spirit which Infested The House of Andrew Mackie in Ringcroft of Stockings, in The Parish of Rerrick, in the Stewartry of Kirkcudbrightshire". Rolls right off the tongue.

Telfer, the four other ministers, and nine other witnesses to the poltergeist put their names to the writings, claiming it was all absolutely true and recounted exactly as they had seen it happen.

What Was The Trouble?

What was tormenting the Mackie family and the McNaughts before them?

By definition; a poltergeist is a ghost or spirit that causes physical harm, loud noises, and destruction of objects. The name even comes from the German "noisy ghost", and The Trouble certainly fits that description perfectly. But what reason would a poltergeist have to haunt Ringcroft Farm?

Poltergeists are thought to be created as a result of a violent or unjust death. Could someone have been murdered on the farm before these families moved in? Or even on the land before a farm even stood there?

Was The Trouble put there by a curse? The Mackie family and a previous owner found items that certainly could have been used for dark magick. But who would have placed these items here and why? As it happened to more than one family, it seems more like a grudge against the farm rather than whoever was living in it. Even after the Mackie family removed the weird objects they found, The Trouble continued to torment them. Were these items unrelated, as unusual as they were?

The Trouble was also able to predict that its reign of terror would last only four more days. From its last time speaking to Mr. Mackie to its apparent exorcism in the cowshed it was indeed exactly four days. Did The Trouble have the power of prescience, or had it already decided it would leave at this time for reasons that were its own? Its grand finale of evil was certainly burning down the farmhouse. Strangely coincidental that it would leave at the same time a large group prayer was taking place however.

Was The Trouble an entity that resides on the land, and had existed since far before a farm was built there? Could The Ringcroft be one of those locations on the thin part of the veil between this world and another?

If so, should anyone ever decide to buy this old land with a dead tree on it and build a home there, they may get far more than they bargained for.

Strangely, The Ringcroft Poltergeist shares many similarities with one of America's most famous poltergeists: The Bell Witch. Though the Bell Witch Haunting happened over 100 years later, both stories feature a family being tormented by a malevolent and invisible spirit in a farmhouse. The Trouble and The Bell Witch also share a few favourite tricks. The Bell Witch enjoyed making noises, pulling sheets from beds while people were asleep, and hitting people with invisible objects. While it would be a stretch to say that The Trouble and The Bell Witch are the same entity, (The Bell Witch went as far as murder while The Trouble was (possibly) a bit more tame) I think it's fair to say they would definitely be friends. Maybe they hang out and trade haunting advice on the astral plane.

Whoever, or whatever, caused The Trouble to inhabit this farm and torment those living and working there, there is no denying it was a very real menace for the Mackie family. One that caused them nothing but problems and eventually destroyed their home and livelihood.

The Flannan
Lighthouse Mystery

When it comes to "best locations for spooky goings on", lighthouses are pretty far up the list.

Usually miles from anything, totally isolated, and the only other people for company are your fellow lighthouse keepers, it's a location perfect for gothic horror. But what if the lighthouse was on a rocky, jagged island far out at sea? And what if that island had a strange history? And what if there was no way off, apart from a ship that only arrived every few weeks? It certainly creates a foreboding atmosphere. With this in mind, it's no surprise that the lighthouse on Flannan Isles is home to one of the most famous mysteries in Scotland.

A Dark Lighthouse

On the 15th of December 1900, the Archtor, an American ship sailing from Philadelphia to a port in Leith, noticed something strange on the Flannan isles; a small group of islands 20 miles off the Isle of Lewis: there was no light coming from the lighthouse on Eilean Mòr.

As the weather was particularly bad as they passed the island, the captain made a note of this in his logbook. His thinking was perhaps that the light had become damaged and the lighthouse keepers were unable to repair it safely due to the strong winds, or maybe didn't even have the parts, tools or know-how to fix whatever problem had occurred.

When the ship docked in Leith 3 days later, they informed the Northern Lighthouse Board of what they had seen. Or rather, what they had not seen.

The Lighthouse Board sent out the ship Hesperus to Flannan on the 20th of December to see what the issue was. Along with the ship's captain; Jim Harvie, and his crew, also onboard was relief lighthouse keeper Joseph Moore. At any time there were three lighthouse keepers in the lighthouse at Flannan, with another relief keeper on shore. These men would rotate every few weeks so that one man would get some time off. In the lighthouse on Flannan at this time were James Ducat, Thomas Marshall, and William MacArtur.

A Silent Lighthouse

Bad weather and rough seas kept the ship from docking at the high cliffs of the island, so captain Harvie tried to get the keepers' attention in any other way he could. He repeatedly blew the ship's loud horn, both to alert the men that a ship was here and to try and get some response to signal that they were okay. No response came. As unlikely as it seemed, maybe the men couldn't hear the boat's horn over the wind.

Captain Harvie then sent up a flare. The men in the lighthouse would definitely see this, and would have their own flares they could send up in reply. Again, there was no response.

Finally, on the 26th of December, relief lighthouse keeper Moore was able to disembark the ship on the East-landing place and make his way up the stone steps carved into the cliffs of Flannan. As the sea was still rough, the Hesperus stayed undocked to avoid it being smashed against the rocks. Moore approached the lighthouse all alone.

When Moore reached the lighthouse, there was no one to greet him. This was his first clue that something was amiss, as any time a keeper came back to the lighthouse to let another go ashore they all met outside.

As he approached the lighthouse proper, he came to the entry gate. It was closed, something else that Moore noted as unusual. Moore went straight to the living quarters at the foot of the lighthouse. It was empty. In the kitchen, a meal had been set out and not eaten. A single chair at the kitchen table had been toppled over. Moore noticed that the living quarters must have been empty for days, as the ashes in the fireplace were cold. Before he left he also noticed that the clock on the wall had curiously stopped.

Feeling uneasy, but still hoping to find his coworkers, Moore made his way through the living quarters to the sleeping area.

Again, no sign of life, but the beds were ominously unmade, as if the lighthouse keepers had been woken up suddenly and had to rush to some emergency before they could do anything else. Moore, now sure that something terrible had happened, went back down the cliff steps and signalled Hesperus for help.

Captain Harvie sent two sailors to Flannan to assist Moore. Moore explained what he had found and all three went back up the cliffs to investigate the actual lighthouse. They found no sign of the missing men there either. They did find that the lamps had been recently cleaned and refilled. They also found two sets of oilskins missing, which suggested that one of the missing men had gone out without wearing his. Not something a lighthouse keeper would reasonably do, especially in the bad weather of the days previous.

Certain that the 3 men were nowhere to be found in or around the lighthouse, Moore and the seamen returned to the Hesperus.

Back onboard, Moore explained everything he had seen and found to Captain Harvie. The Captain decided to leave Moore and three of his crew on the island, to search and maybe even try to repair the light, while he returned to Leith to report what they found at the lighthouse. Surely they were overjoyed to be left totally alone on the mysterious island of disappearing lighthouse keepers without even a working bulb to keep them company.

As the four men waited for Harvie and the Hesperus to return, they decided to search the rest of the island. Whether they thought they were actually alive somewhere on the rock, or whether they just wanted something to keep their minds off the possibility of themselves disappearing next is unknown.

The men had landed on the East side and found nothing out of the ordinary there, but there was a second landing platform on the West of the island. They set out to search this area as it was the only place left they could think that the lighthouse keepers could have gone.

Investigating & Investigations

On the West of the island they predictably found no trace of the men, but things here were definitely out of the ordinary.

From what Moore and the seamen could gather, it seemed like this platform had been hit badly by the recent storm. A box full of supplies, which would normally be safely secured, was out in the open; smashed, with its contents littering the area. An iron railing had been damaged badly, twisted and bent out of shape. A large boulder, estimated to weigh well over a ton, had been moved.

This platform also had a crane for loading and unloading supplies from ships. This crane was undamaged and secured, but had the lighthouse keepers left the safety of their building in the wild storm to try and secure this crane to prevent it from being damaged or blown into the sea? Could they have, during their efforts, been swept into the waters themselves?

Upon his return, this was Captain Harvie's theory. His theory was expanded by the Lighthouse Board's superintendent—Robert Muirhead—in his investigation when he arrived on the island on December 29th.

Muirhead theorised that, judging by the two missing oilskins, Marshall and Ducat had gone out into the bad weather towards the West landing platform with the goal of securing the crane there, only to be washed into the sea by a freak wave, or even blown into the water by a powerful gust. When some time had passed, Muirhead thought, MacArthur headed out to find them, neglecting to put on his own oilskins. When he arrived at the platform, he suffered the same fate.

Alternative Theories

Many have poked holes in this *official* explanation, however.

Some have said that the chances of two insanely large, freak waves hitting the same island so close together is unlikely. They go on to say that all men meeting their fates to waves of this nature is simply outside the laws of probability, unless these lighthouse keepers had some curse placed on them. These naysayers also go on to question the remaining oilskin.

When Marshall and Ducat did not return from the West landing platform, the doubters of the official explanation thought it unlikely that MacArthur would have gone out after them as he would have known the dangers. Even if the man had decided to go after the two other lighthouse keepers, driven on by friendship, it makes no sense that he wouldn't wear the proper gear for the excursion. Ducat would have known that going out without his oilskin would have made his mission all the more deadly.

Some doubt that the men even left the lighthouse and headed for the landing platform. They argue that the men would have had the crane secured in advance. This is backed up by the fact that the crane was not damaged in the storm. Others have pointed to the experience of the lighthouse keepers. They had between 5 and 20 years of lighthouse work each. They would have known not to head out in that weather to save a crane that was, by all accounts, already safely secured.

If these men weren't killed by giant rogue waves while trying to save a crane, what happened to them?

Years after the events of the Flannan Lighthouse, entries from a logbook kept by Marshall surfaced. These entries spoke of a storm and, eerily, of the other two men weeping and praying. It reads like a Gothic horror by the likes of Poe, and seems to hint that something very strange was going on, and the possibility of murderous madness descending on the lighthouse keepers.

As interesting and cinematically appealing these logbook entries are, they have all but been discounted as fakes. No logbook being found was mentioned at the time, it has never been officiated, and is believed to be the work of some unknown author who was either inspired by the mystery or attempting to add to it.

Although it wasn't the direct inspiration, it's hard to imagine that Robert Eggers didn't have this story and these logbooks in mind while he was writing the 2019 film *The Lighthouse*.

Even with the logbook most likely never actually existing, the theory of murder is still prominent and perhaps not too unbelievable.

William MacArthur was known by many to be a man with an explosive temper and was no stranger to violence. Could MacArthur, while stuck indoors due to the storm, have had a falling out with the other two men? Could he have murdered them, thrown their bodies off the cliffs, and then when realising the gravity of what he had done thrown himself off as well?

It doesn't explain the missing two oilskins. What if the fight had happened outside of the lighthouse, with two of the men wearing their oilskins, where either the double-murder suicide happened, or all men somehow managed to fall to their deaths?

Alternative Alternative Theories

As with most mysteries, there are theories that are slightly less human and a bit more paranormal.

Some have claimed that the men were devoured by a massive sea monster. Others, that they were swept up by a giant thunderbird, taken to its nest, and eaten. These two theories have been dismissed by most as "silly". Although, a paranormal explanation may still be possible.

Many referred to Flannan as "the other country". They believed that a very strange presence resided on Eilean Mòr. The main reason for people other than lighthouse keepers to visit the island was its chapel, built in the 7th century. This chapel was said to have a very unusual and strong aura. People who were not religious and had never prayed before would, when visiting the island, drop down in worship. Strange customs inexplicably grew around this chapel, including crawling around it on one's hands and knees.

Rumour had it that seamen from Lewis would not stay overnight on Eilean Mòr, no matter the cause. Farmers would often ferry their sheep to the island to graze, but they, too, refused to stay the night. The reason for this is unknown, but some great fear seems to be the explanation. Could the chapel have harnessed the power of some ancient entity that exists on the island that somehow played into these men's disappearance, and the fear from nearby sailors?

Alien abduction has also been suggested. The clock that had stopped is a common occurrence in abduction stories, usually happening to an abductee's watch or to a clock in their home that they are taken from. Could these lighthouse keepers have been abducted by a UFO and never returned?

A strange report from another ship in the vicinity of Flannan on the same night the Archtor noticed there was no light coming from the lighthouse may, in retrospect, offer a terrifying explanation.

Sailors of the Fair Wind saw a ship sailing towards Flannan. The captain tried to hail this boat, but got no reply. The crew of the Fair Wind rushed to get a look at this boat as it cut in front of theirs. They described the ship as looking like a viking longboat, with men pulling large oars. The seamen on board were described as entirely pale. Almost ghostly. And they seemed entirely unaware of the presence of the Fair Wind. The sailors were sure they were looking at a ghost ship.

A strange and eerie sight for sure, worthy of a story all on its own. But when considering that it was spotted on the very same day that the lighthouse was seen without light, it seems too strange to be mere coincidence.

Could this phantom viking longboat have been drawn to the island by whatever presence dwelled in the ancient chapel? And could the spirits of ancient vikings have made land then invaded the lighthouse? Could these ghosts have killed the men there and then and thrown their bodies to the waves? Or could they have brought them back to their ship, and sailed them off to whatever paranormal realm they had come from? But why would the entity do this? Could it have been angered by the men not visiting the chapel, not breaking down and praying to it?

Whether you believe that these men were whisked away in a storm, or that one of them was driven to murder, or that an evil presence drew a ghost ship to the island, that they were eaten whole by a sea monster, or abducted by extraterrestrials, it's likely that we'll never truly know what happened to the Flannan lighthouse keepers.

Netta & Iona

An isolated location, a cast of strange characters, a bizarre death, connections to the supernatural, and an enduring mystery.

No, I'm not describing the plot to a cult David Lynch TV show, but an actual event on a Scottish island. While there is no Black Lodge, people talking backwards, owls, or damn fine coffee here, it comes with its own surrealness. Surrealness that could surpass even the weirdest of Mr. Lynch's cinematic masterpieces. By the end of this chapter I think you'll agree that this is definitely a case for Special Agent Dale Cooper.

Saint Columba & Nessie

Iona is an island off the Western coast of Scotland. It is incredibly small, not just in size, but in population too. It is barely three and half miles long and currently fewer than 200 people live on it. Despite this, its graveyard is the final resting place of many Scottish kings, including the actual MacBeth.

It is ancient in history, having been settled as a holy island by Saint Columba when he landed there in 563 and built an abbey where himself and many monks could worship. Columba, by a nice bit of synchronicity, has a connection to the mysterious in Scotland that goes far beyond the island of Iona and involves the country's most famous cryptid.

During a trip to mainland Scotland in 565, the saint performed one of his many miracles while visiting a Pictish king. After arriving on the shores of Loch Ness by ferry, Columba found some men preparing to bury one of their friends. They told him that he had been killed by a monster in the loch while swimming. Columba, being the saint that he was, decided that he couldn't simply pass through while a murderous beast attacked locals with impunity. He engaged in the first and, to date only, Saint Versus Kaiju battle.

Columba asked one of his followers who had joined him on his trip to swim across the loch. The follower, likely unaware he was about to be used as Nessie bait, obeyed Columba and went for a very cold swim. Soon enough, they spotted the Loch Ness Monster. It had taken the (very obvious) bait and was speeding towards the poor swimmer. Columba stepped forward into the loch, called upon the power of God, and commanded the creature to stop its attack and leave at once. The monster stopped just metres from the swimming monk and descended into the depths of the loch, and possibly back through whatever tear in the veil it had slithered through, and was imprisoned there by command of a true superpowered saint.

A prison it was perhaps held in until its magical bonds were loosened by a ritual performed in an old hunting lodge near the loch by an occultist some many hundreds of years later.

Even outside of Christianity though, Iona has a vast history of folklore and Paganism, and to this day is still considered an immensely spiritual location. But spirituality is not always harmless, and in 1929 Iona was the setting of a young woman's unexplained and possibly occult related death.

Netta & The Occult

Marie Emily Fornario, or Netta to her friends, was born in Cairo in 1897 to an Egyptian mother and an Italian father. After her mother died and her father left her, she was sent to live with her grandfather in London. After his death in 1909, he left her a sum of money in his will: £12,000, quite a large amount back then. This gave her the freedom she needed to travel and experience the things she had always wanted to.

After briefly living in Italy, she returned to the UK in 1922 and took an interest in the newly reinvigorated occult movement. Shortly after, she was initiated into The Order of Alpha and Omega, an offshoot of The Hermetic Order of The Golden Dawn that remained loyal to their original founder: Samuel Mathers.

Mathers had founded The Golden Dawn in 1887 with two others, William Woodman and William Westcott. It was a secret society dedicated to the study and practice of the occult, metaphysics and the paranormal.
The Golden Dawn started to experience problems in 1898, and when a certain new magician and occultist joined—the one and only Aleister Crowley—tensions only increased. Crowley brought his own ideas to the group, and the inflated egos of the founding members coupled by Crowley just being Crowley caused many arguments. Mathers' friendship with Crowley caused a split in the leadership, with Mathers and Crowley on one side and the Williams' (or The Willies, as I like to call them) on the other.

The leadership of The Golden Dawn broke up in 1903, with Mathers founding his new society The Order of Alpha and Omega, and inviting Golden Dawn members who were still loyal to him to join.

Crowley did not join The Order of Alpha and Omega and instead, like the Fleetwood Mac song; went his own way, and formed his own order 1904: Thelema.

By this point Crowley and Mathers had fallen out badly. Their relationship as master and student soured as the two became vicious enemies, using their magical powers to fight each other, much like Obi-Wan and Anakin. Mathers reportedly summoned a vampire to attack Crowley. I can't say Mathers thought his plan through very well; getting bitten by a vampire and turning into one seems like something Crowley would have loved. His lifestyle wouldn't have changed much: he'd still be hanging out in the dark, making dramatic speeches, wearing a cape, and occasionally drinking blood.

In retaliation, Crowley summoned psychic hounds to attack Mathers. This went back and forth for some time, on and off, until they both got bored. Samuel died in 1918, allowing Crowley to crown himself victor.

Netta quickly became fascinated with the teachings of Mathers' new order, now almost twenty years into its existence.

During this time, Netta would impress her friends and those

around her with her new spirituality, occult knowledge, and strange rituals. Eventually, Netta told her maid that she would be travelling to the island of Iona to perform one of her magical rituals and that she wasn't sure how long it would take, so she would be staying indefinitely.

What she actually planned to do on Iona is unknown, but given the island's ancient history and spiritual past, it could be any number of things. One theory is that she intended to perform a rite to bring peace to a fairy woman that had been burned alive by monks in the distant past. Others theorise she was simply there to study and learn more about the fae, which she believed would be abundant on the island.

Netta Arrives on Iona

When Netta arrived on Iona, the locals took an instant liking to her. Her appearance and metropolitan style made her stand out from the rest of the population and they took her in as something of a fun novelty. This was added to when the locals would spot her going into trances, walking the moors at night, and attempting to contact the spirits near Loch Stoanaig. She had no problem finding a place to stay among the friendly locals and took up lodgings with the MacRae family.

Netta got on particularly well with Mrs. MacRae, and told her that she could communicate with spirits by falling into one of her famous trances, and not long before travelling to the island she had fallen into one of these trances for a full week. She told Mrs. MacRae that if she should see her in such a trance, she should not send for a doctor and just leave her to it. Mrs. MacRae agreed and thought it to be just another of Netta's quirky eccentricities.

Soon after this, Mrs. MacRae and her family started to become increasingly concerned for Netta. She would often go missing for hours at a time, even spending an entire night on the moors claiming she had gotten lost. She told the family that she had been receiving troubling messages from the spirit world while in trance. She claimed she had seen what she described as a "rudderless boat" fly across the sky (a flying object that she couldn't... identify?), and that she was being psychically attacked.

Mrs. MacRae suspected Netta was simply losing her mind, until one day she entered Netta's room and discovered that all of her silver jewellery had mysteriously turned black, seemingly overnight. Mrs. MacRae was sure this was a side effect of some occult attack on Netta.

Netta Disappears

On the morning of 17th November 1929, Mrs. MacRae found Netta in an unusual mood. She was distant, restless, muttering, and messily packing all of her possessions into bags. She told Mrs. MacRae that she needed to leave the island as soon as possible. Mrs. MacRae told her that it was a Sunday and that the ferry, the only way off the island, wouldn't be in operation until Monday.

Netta ignored her, and went to the port anyway, possibly hoping to pay a local fisherman for a lift. She returned to the MacRae house several hours later, upset that she had no choice but to stay on the island until morning. She went to her room without speaking to anyone.

Some hours later, Netta emerged from her room, seemingly in a better mood. She informed the family she was going on one of her usual walks. She hadn't returned by the time the MacRaes went to bed, but this wasn't unusual: Netta often stayed out late just walking around the old historic sites on the island.

She still hadn't returned by the next morning. The family waited a couple of hours, thinking she had maybe just gotten lost on the moors again, but when she still had not returned some time later, they formed a search party. Due to Netta's popularity around the island, many joined the search.

They combed the beaches and surrounding rocks, fearing she may have fallen into the ocean from a steep cliffside in the dark. Finding nothing, they turned their attention to the moorlands, knowing it to be one of Nettas favourite locations to walk, but again found nothing. They searched for the whole of the 18th of November, but found no sign of Netta.

A Body Found

The next afternoon, on the 19th of November, two local men searched the remains of an ancient village by the shores of Loch Stoanaig, which Netta was fond of visiting. On a nearby hillside they found her body.

She was laying atop a small mound, wearing only a black cloak, with a blackened silver necklace around her neck, and a small silver dagger lying near her hand. Underneath her body, a large cross had been carved into the earth. Her body was covered in scratch marks, and her bare feet were blistered and bloody.

To add more mystery and occult connotations to her death, the mound she was lying on is known as a fairy mound. Fairy mounds, or fairy forts, are the remains of stone circles, ringforts or other prehistoric dwellings grown over with plant life, and are thought to contain druidic magic. There are many paranormal stories that involve these fairy mounds throughout history.

A coroner concluded that her cause of death was exposure to the elements and did not think any foul play was involved. He couldn't place her time of death either, other than it being within the last two days.
Exposure was certainly the most likely cause of Netta's death. Being out on a November night in Scotland wearing nothing but a thin robe is definitely a good way to get yourself killed, but ruling out foul play caused much speculation and debate. Netta was familiar with how low the temperature could drop at night, something she probably learned the hard way from her night lost on the moors.

It seems strange then that she would purposely dress in a way she knew was inadequate for the weather. Stranger still, there were many people on the island that could have given her shelter if she had simply knocked on their door and asked. The coroner's judgement seemed to be that Netta had simply dressed this way, then laid down to die. No one who knew Netta would accept this explanation, and pointed to her injured feet as proof she was running from someone or something.

So what was Netta doing out there, dressed in robes? Who, or what, could have been pursuing her? And was it responsible for her death?

What Happened to Netta?

She was not wearing the robe she was found in when she left the MacRae home, and some theorise these were the robes followers of The Order of Alpha and Omega would wear while performing a ritual. Was Netta preparing for a ritual? Was she in the process of performing one? Or had she already performed her ritual? Did the ritual go wrong, or backfire?

If she was indeed on Iona to try and bring peace to a fairy lady burned alive by monks, is it possible she broke through to the spirit realm but instead encountered the spirits of these ancient Christian monks who felt the same way about Netta and her beliefs as they did about the fairy lady? It's most likely this "fairy lady" was some sort of Pagan or Druid and would have shared many beliefs with Netta. Some occultists said the cross shape cut into the ground would have been used in a ritual to contact another realm.

Some say the marks on her feet are proof that Netta was running from something. But who would have been chasing her? As she was so beloved on Iona, it seems unlikely any of the locals would have had any grudge against her, and certainly not enough to warrant murdering her.

Is it possible Netta was indeed running from something, but not a physical presence? She had been complaining of receiving psychic attacks for some time, even claiming they were coming from someone on the island. Was she performing a ritual to try and block these attacks, or even fight back, but whoever she was fighting against was too strong for her?

Members of The Order of Alpha and Omega have said that Netta would attempt magick that was far out of her depth and beyond her understanding. But who on the island would possess the ability to psychically attack someone? Unless it wasn't a living person at all.

Could the spirit of a follower of a long dead religion have taken issue with Netta and her practices and attacked her from beyond the grave? Nettas desire to open doors between worlds certainly would have made her an easy target for any disgruntled spirits on the other side.

Could the psychic attacks have come from within The Order of Alpha and Omega itself?

When Netta joined the Order, she was taught by the wife of Samuel Mathers; Moina Mathers. They got along well until Moina accused Netta of revealing the society's occult secrets and had her expelled from the Order. If she believed Netta was still revealing these secrets, or just held a grudge, would she attempt to attack and even kill Netta through occult means? Some occultists say that the scratches found on her body were consistent with wounds they had seen in psychic attacks previously inflicted by Moina. There was only one problem with this theory: Moina had died sixteen months before Netta.

Could Moina have attacked Netta from beyond the grave? Or could she have left instructions for the Order to take revenge against Netta? If Mathers and Crowley could summon up vampires and demonic hounds to attack each other, it stands to reason that other members of the order would possess similar, if less dramatic, powers.

Crowley himself could famously hold a grudge. He would turn up at ex-followers' homes, sometimes as long as decades after he last saw them to threaten them with curses. Did Netta somehow offend Crowley, causing a belated psychic retaliation? Crowley does have his own odd connection to the island. One of the many titles he bestowed upon himself was the incredibly modest "Supreme and Holy King of Ireland, Iona and all the Britains within the Sanctuary of the Gnosis". If Crowley really did consider himself the holy king of Iona, would he have any occult power over it?

Could Netta have been attacked by an actual person, but a person unaware of what they were doing? Could a local of the island have been possessed by paranormal or occult powers and forced to murder Netta?

Netta was buried in the Reilig Odhrain graveyard alongside the old Scottish kings. Engraved on her simple tombstone are the initials M.E.F., the date of her death, and her age: 33 years old.

Those who saw Nettas body said that the look of terror frozen onto her dead face was all the proof they needed that something terrible and unspeakable had come for her in the night. Whether it was physical, psychic, conjured or summoned, or just an entirely ordinary tragedy, something certainly did happen to this young occultist on the ancient and sacred island of Iona.

RIP Netta.

The Livingston Encounter

UFO sightings/encounters are classified by the Close Encounter Scale, created by the legendary J. Allen Hynek. Close Encounters of the First Kind are the most common; these cover just seeing a UFO. The usual report goes something like: a person sees a strange object in the sky, they observe it for a period of time, then the object speeds off or disappears.

A Close Encounter of the Second Kind is when a UFO has some sort of effect on the witness or the area around them. This can include cars breaking down, animals being scared, the witness getting a heat burn, crop circles, and so on.

A Close Encounter of the Third Kind is an underrated Spielberg movie and when a witness actually sees not just a UFO, but also meets the alien/robot/creature/entity inside of it. This is the rarest of the Encounter Scale for obvious reasons.

Sometimes though, there is an encounter that seems to go beyond Hynek's Encounter Scale. Sometimes someone experiences something that seems totally unquantifiable and doesn't fit into any of the boxes. For example, what if the object seen isn't in the sky? And what if it doesn't just leave? What if it attacks?

Robert & The Balls

On November 9, 1979, a UFO encounter occurred in Livingston that put Scotland on the extraterrestrial map. This was an encounter so strange and believable that it began a massive investigation into UFOs in Scotland, an area that had been somewhat ignored by investigators to that point. An encounter so bizarre and unexplainable that investigators, sceptics and believers still look into this case, only to come away empty handed.

At 11:00 am on the morning of November 9, 1979, 60-year-old Robert Taylor was walking his dog through Dechmont Law, a wooded area on the edge of Livingston. As he walked through the woods, Robert and the canine came into a clearing. What he saw here stopped him in his dog walking tracks.

Twelve feet in front of him, in the centre of the clearing, there was a large spherical object about six metres in diameter. The spherical object was a metallic dark grey, with a rim around its middle. The object didn't move, but as Robert slowly approached it, two smaller spherical objects dropped out of the large object. The balls that dropped had small spikes all around them and reminded Robert of naval mines. Soon after the balls dropped, Robert smelled an odd odour that he described as being similar to burning rubber.

The small balls approached Robert Taylor and he attempted to flee. As he turned to run, Robert realised he had lost the use of his legs. He was frozen in place. The balls attacked Robert. Or more specifically, they attacked his trousers. Why they did this is unknown, but some theorise that the alien intelligence controlling these balls mistook the trousers for the dominant life form on the planet and reacted with extreme hostility.

As these extraterrestrial trouser troublers were making short work of Robert's leg garments, the unpleasant smell in the air became stronger and stronger. Robert inexplicably passed out and fell to the ground. Just before he entirely lost consciousness, he was aware that his trousers were being grabbed from the bottom and pulled by something. Luckily he was wearing a belt.

Robert awoke twenty minutes later, and all three of the strange objects were gone. Robert's trousers were now totally decimated, his legs had some small cuts and bruises, and he was several feet away from where he had passed out. It seemed as if while Robert was out cold, the small balls had tried to drag him toward the larger one, perhaps as an attempted abduction.

During this whole ordeal, Roberts' dog stayed by his side, barking at the attacking balls and guarding her passed out master. Perhaps the actions of this brave pooch are what deterred the intergalactic spheres and saved Robert from a fate far worse than just a ruined pair of trousers.

Robert recomposed himself and left the woods. He got back to his truck which inexplicably would not start, leaving him no choice but to walk all the way home. A trip his dog enjoyed far more than he. When he arrived home in a dishevelled state, wearing tattered trousers, his wife was understandably concerned. She asked what was wrong, Robert told her he had been attacked by something from outer space. After he explained what had happened, his wife phoned the police.

The Police Investigate

The police didn't exactly believe his story of being attacked in the local woods by strange spheres from beyond the stars, and thought it was far more likely he was attacked by a gang of feral teenagers or forest dwelling miscreants. Though why either would disguise themselves as xenomorphic marbles was admittedly a mystery.

Whether terrestrial or extraterrestrial, the police decided to investigate the clearing Robert was attacked in. When they arrived, they were surprised to find evidence that backed up Robert's story. They found marks on the ground and an indentation in the grass that looked like a ladder had lain where Robert claimed the large sphere was.

There were also tracks left where the smaller balls had travelled, and larger tracks where Robert had been pulled towards the bigger ball. They also found indents in the ground, as if some vehicle with treads had driven through. What made this stranger was that the tracks and small holes left by the objects just vanished, as if picked up from above. No other similar tracks could be found anywhere nearby.

The police went to the nearby forestry company, who also happened to be Robert's employers, to see if they had any machinery or equipment that could have caused these tracks and markings. The police may have thought that Robert could have borrowed something from work in order to create fake UFO markings. The police inspected everything the company had, but could find nothing that matched up to the tracks created, and could think of no way that forestry equipment could be removed from the clearing without leaving any trails (the company did not own a helicopter, plane, hot air balloon, blimp, etc).

The police then took Robert's trousers (the ones that were ripped during the encounter, not the ones he was currently wearing). They were sent for examination, but as this was the late 70s, and long before the wonders of CSI and CSI: Miami, there was little they could learn from Roberts trousers that the label couldn't tell them. However, they were able to deduce that the rips on the legs were caused by some sort of hook ripping into them and then being pulled upwards. This discounted the theory that they were torn on a barbed wire fence while Robert was travelling home after the encounter. The trousers are now owned by a UFO investigator. Lucky him.

The police had to admit that something truly strange did happen to Robert Taylor in these woods. Many possible explanations were put forward to try and rationally explain what had happened to Robert.

Theories

Some say Robert simply saw Venus. What this was meant to explain exactly is unclear. Saying that seeing a moderately bright planet in the morning sky would make Robert think he had seen a UFO and been attacked by strange objects that came out of it doesn't make a lot of sense.

A more sensible theory is the possibility that Robert had an attack of temporal lobe epilepsy. This would explain Robert hallucinating, smelling an unexpected odour, being frozen in place, and passing out. It does not explain the physical evidence of the ripped trousers and the marks left in the ground however. Some suggested that a water company may have left pipes in the clearing, which could explain the indentations, but no one from the company has ever come forward to say they left pipes there and, given the media attention the encounter was given, it seems unlikely they would have not heard about it — and, we still have the matter of the mysterious trousers to contend with.

Backing up Robert's story, a few people did see strange lights in the sky the night before his encounter. A woman was making her way to work when she saw a silver light that appeared to be descending on Dechmont Law. The same object (or a similar one) was also seen by a lorry driver from a different angle. These sightings alone might not be extraordinary, but when paired with what happened to Robert the next morning, it certainly adds some believability to his story.

Robert Taylor was a well liked member of the community. No one that knew him believed he would lie or make up a fantastical story. Robert never changed his story, and stuck to it until the day he died. He never tried to make money from, or exploit, his encounter.

Legacy

Years later, Taylor's encounter in Dechmont Law has passed into ufology legend. It is not only one of the most researched and famous cases of a UFO encounter in Scotland, but in the world. Retellings of the event can be found in countless books on the UFO phenomenon, it can be heard discussed on numerous podcasts, and has even been featured in TV shows and documentaries.

In the 90s a plaque was erected in the clearing, letting paranormal tourists know exactly where the UFO balls attacked Robert. Later, an entire country trail was dedicated to the Livingston Encounter, allowing visitors to walk through Dechmont Law right to the clearing. None of these visitors have, to date, seen what Robert saw that day in 1979.

What Were The Balls?

But what did Robert see? What were the strange balls? Were they indeed UFO crafts? Piloted by tiny extraterrestrial creatures, each only a few inches in height? In most alien encounters the beings are described as being roughly human sized, sometimes a little taller or shorter. Is there any reason why ETs shouldn't be tiny? If these particular creatures piloting the balls came from a planet that resulted in them evolving to be this size, why not? If aliens are coming from a variety of different planets, why would they all be a uniform size or appearance?

If the balls were not being driven by little (tiny) green men, then perhaps they were being controlled remotely. Could the balls have been operated by beings onboard a UFO somewhere above in orbit, or maybe even outside of our solar system? Perhaps the balls were like drones, sent by aliens to scout out locations on Earth before they make their way here and land personally? Perhaps before any sighting of a landed UFO, these balls have been in the area beforehand . Had these balls not encountered Robert while he was out walking his dog, could Dechmont Law have had some more organic visitors shortly after?

Livingston also falls into The Falkirk Triangle, along with Bonnybridge. Whether Zalus had a hand in Robert's attack is unknown.

The Egyptian Bone

When we think of an Egyptian Curse, we usually think of explorers in the early 1900's opening the tomb of a long dead pharaoh, taking some sacred object, breaking the rules of an ancient religion, and one by one being punished through cruel and unusual deaths.

While this may seem like the plot of an old black and white horror movie, there are reports of just this happening. Archaeologists and tomb robbers (not to be confused with tomb raiders) alike have been subjected to bad luck, strange mishaps, illness, and even death. While many have explained away these supposed curses as simple coincidence, the result of bacteria trapped in the tombs, and elaboration to create a good story, there is some evidence for curses being placed on the resting places of the ancient Egyptians. An inscription found in one tomb translated to a threat directed towards anyone who entered. It read that any intruder "would have an end made for them", and "the fear of the pharaoh shall be cast into them."

A curse just like this may have befallen a Scottish couple during a misguided sightseeing tour.

An Unlikely Souvenir

The year was 1936 and Sir Alexander Hay Seton was holidaying in

Egypt with his wife Zeyla. Obviously they wanted to take in the sights and went on a tour of the pyramids, the Valley of Kings, and even the tomb of Tutankhamen. Alexander found these locations unimpressive at best, perhaps thinking that nothing could rival the magnificent castle and Arthur's Seat back home in Edinburgh.

Their guide, sensing that Alexander wanted something more, offered to bring them to a newly unearthed tomb. In the tomb, he said, was a body that predated the ancient Egyptian practices of mummification. Zeyla, enjoying their tour, eventually managed to talk Alexander into visiting this new tourist attraction. Alexander later said that even before entering the tomb that he had a very bad feeling about it.

The couple descended into the tomb and were greeted (not literally) by a several thousand year old skeleton. From the items still intact in the tomb, Alexander guessed that the skeleton was female and was likely a princess or priestess in life. After a quick look around, Alexander left the tomb for a smoke while Zeyla stayed behind. A few minutes later she emerged and joined her husband, carrying a souvenir. She has taken a small piece of bone that had fallen off the skeleton. This was before the time of gift shops and novelty fridge magnets. Alexander described the bone as looking "like a digestive biscuit". Their tour had obviously made him hungry.

They took the bone back home to their house in Learmouth Gardens in Edinburgh. Alexander had the bone placed in a small glass box and displayed it on his dining room table. Soon after they arrived home from Egypt, they had friends over for dinner and drinks to welcome them back (while a piece of a dead person lay encased in the middle of the table. Classy!). When they were all in the dining room, suddenly part of the roof broke off and came crashing down, missing Alexander, Zeyla, and their guests by inches.

No reason could be found for why part of the dining room roof would suddenly fall, the building was well constructed and showed no damage or fault. They wrote this off as an unfortunate mystery, had the roof repaired, and moved on.

The Bone Attacks

A few nights later, while Alexander and Zeyla were in bed, the couple's nanny came to their bedroom complaining of a strange noise coming from inside the dining room. Alexander knew no one else was in the building and suspected an intruder. He burst into the dining room, ready to subdue whoever he found, but the room was totally empty. Alexander assumed that the nanny had just been hearing things, thought no more of it, and went back to bed.

The next morning when he entered the dining room, the table had been flipped over and the small glass case containing the bone lay nearby. This shocked Alexander, but he rationalised it by saying the vibrations of passing traffic must have caused the table to jump several feet in the air, flip upside down, and land the wrong way up. That's some heavy traffic! What's more, no one was awoken by any noise during the night. Surely a table flipping over would have caused a crash loud enough to wake even the heaviest sleepers.

Strange happenings continued in the house, leading Alexander to believe there was a burglar hiding somewhere inside, waiting for the right moment to strike.

Footsteps were heard from around the house, particularly on the stairs, but no one else was in the house that could be causing these noises. When a nephew of Alexanders was staying over, he claimed to have seen an unknown lady in the house dressed in unusual and foreign-looking clothing. Whether this nephew knew about the Egyptian bone and just imagined an appropriate looking spectre to match is unknown.

Alexander believed that his nephew had indeed seen someone in the house, but not a ghost. He was sticking firmly to his live-in burglar theory. He believed this woman was after his antique snuff boxes, and decided to stay up into the early morning in an attempt to catch her in the act.

Alexander stayed awake for hours, but saw and heard nothing. He eventually went to bed, but it wasn't long before he was awoken by sounds coming from the dining room and his wife's scream. He bolted out of bed and rushed to the room, ready to catch his burglar. He threw open the door and found the room a total mess. It looked like it had been raided, but nothing was stolen and there was no sign of anyone entering or leaving.

Books were grabbed from their shelves and scattered around the room, chairs had been violently flung about the place, the table was once again overturned, and nearby was the Egyptian bone; curiously outside of its glass prison.

Alexander was starting to believe that the unusual occurrences in the house may not have a rational explanation like he initially thought, and Zeyla was convinced that there was something supernatural at work. They decided to clear the room, perhaps thinking it was merely the dining room that was the problem. They moved all the furniture to their sitting room and the bone came along on its table.

All was quiet for a couple of nights, until Alexander and Zeyla were once again awoken by loud noises and banging - this time coming from the sitting room. They rushed to see what the commotion was, and found the sitting room in much the same condition as the dining room after the recent invisible attack. In the centre of the room was the Egyptian bone.

Is This Thing Cursed?

After struggling to make itself any more obvious, Alexander and Zeyla finally came to the conclusion that the bone itself was causing all these problems. Alexander thought the only solution was to destroy the bone by burning it.

Anyone with even a fleeting interest in the paranormal will tell you that this is just about the worst thing you could possibly do to a cursed or possessed object. Those people would also tell you that stealing a bone from the skeleton of a priestess in an ancient and sacred tomb is also probably something to not do if you want to avoid dire supernatural consequences.

Zeyla talked him out of this idea, and they agreed to hold on to the bone until they could figure out a safe way to dispose of it.

Around this time the story of the cursed bone somehow made its way to an Edinburgh journalist. It was probably told to the journalist by a mutual friend of the Hay Setons', but given its history of spooky abilities we cannot discount the possibility that the bone wrote him a letter itself.

The journalist visited the home in Learmouth Gardens and eventually managed to convince Alexander and Zeyla to let him borrow the bone for a week. They agreed, possibly hoping that if the bone was somewhere else their torment would stop. Unfortunately, while the bone was with the journalist the strange events in the house continued. The sitting room was once again trashed, and the table the bone would usually have sat on was damaged.

The journalist returned the bone and reported that no paranormal activity had happened during his week babysitting (bonesitting) it. It is rumoured that the journalist was later injured in a car accident that some have blamed on the curse, but it seems that the bone was only interested in punishing the two that had taken it from its owner.

With the bone back in their possession and sitting on its usual table, Alexander and Zeyla got back to trying to find a way to break the curse. It was during this time that the nanny once again came to Alexander complaining of loud noises, this time coming from the sitting room.

Alexander, knowing what to expect, went to investigate. The room was once again in a mess, but this time something worse had happened. The table was snapped in two, the glass case was smashed, and the Egyptian bone had broken into five pieces.

After this incident, Alexander and Zeyla decided to tell the local press about their curse. They possibly thought that if it got some media attention, someone might come forward with an explanation and a solution to their problem. According to legend, a journalist that tried to take the bone to study it became very ill until it was returned to the Hay Setons'.

With the bone returned and with no one else willing to take it, Zeyla took the pieces to a doctor who was able to place it back together. The doctor told Zeyla that the bone was likely from the base of the spine. With the bone returned back to its original glory, Zeyla returned home. The bone was placed in a new glass box and placed on a nice new table.

On boxing day Alexander and Zeyla had some friends over for dinner. Stories of the cursed bone had spread around Edinburgh, and their friends obviously wanted to know more about it. The Hay Setons' didn't really want to talk about it, which would have been easier if they didn't have the bone lying in the middle of the table they were sitting around.

After brushing off their guests' questions and trying to move the conversation onto a new subject, the table suddenly leaped into the air and crashed into the wall. The guests screamed, some fainted, some ran from the room, and some even from the house entirely.

After this incident, the story exploded. It was reported all over the country, and even in the United States. Alexander had finally had enough. He returned to his original idea of burning it. He had a priest come over to perform an exorcism on the Egyptian bone and then burned it to ashes.

The curse seemed like it had lifted for a while. There were no more trashed rooms and destroyed tables, but the curse may have become more personal. The Hay Setons' began to suffer health problems and a run of bad luck shortly after the bone was destroyed. Alexander and Zeyla soon got divorced. What happened to Zeyla after this is unknown, but Alexander got married again, divorced again, married a third time, foresaw his own death, then died.

Had the Hay Setons' returned the bone to its owner in Egypt, would the curse have been broken? Or was the damage already done when Zeyla decided to take it as a memento of their holiday?

Did burning the bone exacerbate the problem, giving the curse the power to attack the personal lives of Alexander and Zeyla? Or was the exorcism enough to stop the curse, and everything that happened afterwards just a series of unlucky and unrelated events?

And who did the bone belong to? Perhaps if we knew more about this woman and her place in ancient Egyptian society we might be able to determine why this curse followed stealing part of her skeleton.

The East Kilbride Goblin

Goblins are usually thought of as a fantasy creature, easily pictured chasing the Fellowship of the Ring through the Mines of Moria or being slain by a spotty teenager with a twenty sided die, but there are some accounts of Goblin-like creatures making an appearance in real life.

The most famous goblin encounter is without a doubt the Hopkinsville Encounter. In 1955, a farmhouse in Kentucky was attacked by small, silver, glow-in-the-dark creatures with large eyes and ears. Several people saw these creatures and the police were even called to try and find them, and possibly arrest them for trespassing and causing criminal damage. Ever since, these entities have been known as The Hopkinsville Goblins.

There have however been other reports of normal people encountering strange creatures straight out of a Monster Manual, one of which took place in East Kilbride, Scotland.

A Man & A Goblin

In the 1980s a man known only as Martin — who will not share his last name to remain as anonymous as possible and avoid ridicule — took his dog to a field just outside of East Kilbride for a walk. His dog ran into the treeline chasing something that Martin couldn't quite make out, but he assumed to be a rabbit or a hare.

As his dog continued to chase the unknown animal, Martin caught some glimpses of it. He saw that there was a dark blood red on it. He thought this animal might be injured and whistled for his dog to stop its chase. However, instead of the whistle getting his dog's attention, it caught the attention of the creature the dog was chasing; whistling perhaps sounding similar to its native language.

The creature approached Martin, and as it came out of the treeline, he realised the creature didn't have blood on it; its skin was coloured red. He described it as being the shape of an owl with a round head that sunk deep into its shoulders, and leathery crimson skin. It had no noticeable limbs, and seemed to be hovering or gliding instead of flying. It had no nose, mouth or, for the time being, eyes.

The creature showed no fear and came as close as six feet to Martin. As it looked up at Martin with its faceless head, two large, blue, almond shaped eyes appeared on the creature. The eyes were positioned vertically, rather than horizontally; like human or animal eyes.

Although it bore little to no resemblance to the little green fantasy creatures the name suggests, the first thing Martin could think upon seeing this creature was that it was a goblin. Whether or not this creature was something that could be described as a goblin, Martin was absolutely sure he had seen something that should not exist. A creature not of this world. It was during this time Martin noticed that his dog had gone silent. In fact, it had totally disappeared.

After the goblin stared down Martin for a short period of time it simply turned, floated back into the treeline, and disappeared into the woods. It was at this point that the dog reappeared. Martin quickly left the area, quite shaken by his encounter.

Goblin or Alien?

What did Martin encounter? Was it a goblin? Or was it something else? Dating back to ancient times, humans have reported meetings with creatures they did not believe could exist. During the Victorian era, people reported meeting fantastical creatures like fairies. Viewed through a modern lens though, and with years of UFO research behind us, many of these meetings make more sense as extraterrestrial encounters.

Even the Hopkinsville Goblins, creatures that were far closer to the classic description of a goblin, are now thought to have been alien entities. In fact, these creatures and this encounter are what popularised the term "little green men" (despite them being silver, confusingly!). Could a craft, a UFO, have been nearby? Perhaps using an advanced alien cloaking device to remain unseen, but waiting for the round red pilot to return? Could what Martin encountered have been a creature from another planet?

Or was it a creature from another dimension? Perhaps during his dog's unexplained absence it had fallen through the same wormhole the "goblin" had travelled through. But what was this creature doing here? Had it travelled here intentionally, or did it find its way to our world accidentally? Was this its first visit, or had it been here before? And was this its final visit, or did it return? Has anyone else seen this creature and simply been too embarrassed of ridicule to come forward and report it? It's a fear that almost kept Martin quiet and led to him never disclosing his real identity.

Perhaps if someone was to return to the same area in Kilmarnock at just the right time, during very specific conditions, they might get lucky and arrive just as an interdimensional wormhole briefly opens. And if they are very lucky, they might just catch a glimpse of a creature from another world.

Whether goblin, alien, extradimensional creature, whatever Martin encountered in these East Kilbride woods, it's clear it was certainly something that had a lasting impact on him.

The A70 Abduction

Alien abduction is one of the more terrifying aspects of ufology. The idea of being suddenly plucked from your home, car, or even taken while out for a walk, and having no power to stop your kidnapping or fight back against your extraterrestrial abductors conjures feelings of fear, dread and terror.

From there it only gets worse: finding yourself onboard a strange craft, surrounded by humanoid creatures, and having weird experiments performed on your body. Once you're returned home, you have a gap in your memory. All you know is that there are several hours that you cannot account for and you have strange marks on your body that weren't there before this missing time.

When you're asleep, you have disturbing nightmares of being taken aboard a vessel that cannot possibly exist by creatures that don't look quite human. Then you feel the pain of unfamiliar devices being forced into your skin, and you wake in a cold sweat. Do you decide this is just a recurring nightmare, or do you try to find out more?

It's a story that has been told time and again in UFO lore, with many famous cases following a similar narrative structure. Scotland has its own famous alien abduction case, which rivals even the most famous in the world.

The Thing Above The Road

On the evening of August 17, 1992, two friends were unexpectedly thrown into the world of ufology. When they set out that night, little did they know they would soon be involved in one of Scotland's most famous cases of alien abduction.

The night began innocently enough. Garry Wood was about to leave his home in Edinburgh and head to the village of Tarbrax, about 30 to 45 minutes away, to deliver a satellite TV system to his friend Ian Phillips — very high-tech stuff in 1992. Just as he was about to leave, his other friend, Colin Wright, arrived. Garry had a lot of friends; I guess that's what happens when you don't spend your life writing about aliens, cryptids, and the occult.

Colin decided to join Garry and keep him company on the short drive, a choice he would soon regret. They set off at around 10pm. As they drove along the A70, Colin spotted something in the sky. He pointed it out to Garry, and both men saw a strange craft hovering in place about 20 feet above the road in front of them.

They described it as being a metallic, shiny black, disc shaped object, 40 feet across and completely silent. Though it showed no signs of being aggressive, Wood was terrified. He said he had the feeling that if he stopped the car to get a better look at it, something would "run up and grab him". He accelerated under the object, eager to get far away from it as quickly as he could. As he drove under the craft, a beam of shimmering light shone out from beneath it. The light covered the entire width of the road.

The next thing Garry remembered was being outside of the car in total darkness. After that, Garry remembers being back in the car, on the wrong side of the road, with Colin screaming "Did you see it?" at him.

Garry then drove at speeds of up to 90 mph until he reached Ian's house. He knocked at the door and was shocked when Ian answered and asked "What took you so long?" It was now 12:45; the journey to Ian's house somehow took over three times longer than it should have.

For weeks afterwards, Garry was troubled by terrible nightmares and one morning even woke up to find he had been sleep walking, left his house, and had wandered a mile away from home. As he had also developed severe headaches around this time, he went to his doctor and was given a CT scan, but nothing unusual showed up.

Forgotten Memories

Garry had slowly come to terms that something very strange happened to him and his friend on the A70 that night — something that he could not remember. He convinced Colin to join him for several sessions of hypnotherapy. The men went to Helen Waters, a qualified hypnotherapist, to undergo hypnotic regression to try and find out what had happened in their collective hour or so of missing time.

The story that was slowly revealed by Garry through hypnosis was shocking. Garry described that after the car went under the shiny craft on the A70, the car stopped dead, and Garry felt like he was being electrocuted. He remembered three small humanoid figures approaching the car.

Garry had no memory of leaving his car (though Colin remembered his friend being taken out of the car by the 3 figures and being placed on a levitating stretcher), and the next thing he knew was in a room, presumably on the UFO above. A large humanoid figure, at least six feet tall with translucent grey skin, appeared and spoke to him telepathically while the smaller beings worked around him. It appeared to Garry that the larger being was in charge.

Along with the tall and short Grey aliens, Garry also saw a third type of extraterrestrial onboard. This 3rd ET was also short, but was brown in colour. Also, unlike the Greys, it was not smooth. These beings were wrinkly, with big folds of skin covering their faces. For some reason that Garry could not explain; these brown beings were the ones that caused him the most fear.

Even a fourth entity was spied onboard, but this one wasn't an alien. Or, at least, it didn't *look* like an alien. Garry claimed that in the room he lay in he also saw a man in a suit. As if we needed anymore evidence that the Men in Black are at the very least working with extraterrestrials, if not extraterrestrial in origin themselves.

The aliens, whether grey, brown or suited, seemed to be trying to comfort Garry, as one told him (again telepathically) "I've got a life like yours, but different." Strangely worded, but Garry took this to mean not to be afraid. He asked the alien what it wanted and it replied "Sanctuary. We are already here and we are coming here."

The comfort offered was well needed, as they next subjected Garry to some medical experiments. Garry was stripped and placed on a table. His memories get fuzzy here, but he remembers being totally paralyzed. He saw two objects leading into his chest. He heard a strange humming inside his ear. Most terrifyingly of all though, he remembers a red hot poker-like object being forced into his eye.

During this whole ordeal, Garry had not seen his friend Colin, but he did see another human. He saw a woman who was also being subjected to medical tests. He described her as being also naked, blonde, and in her early 20's.

Garry then remembers seeing a hole in the floor of the room. It was filled with a sticky gel-like substance, and he could see something moving in it. Soon after he saw a thin, grey creature rise out of the gel. He described the creature as very tall. Taller than a human. It had long limbs and was very skinny. Its ribs seemed to be bruised. He said it looked like a skeleton with flesh around it, the skin tight to its bones. It had a large head, with two large dark eyes that did not look human. It looked like some sort of inhumanoid ghoul.

The next thing Garry remembered was being back in the car, on the wrong side of the road, with Colin shouting at him.

Another Side of The Story

Colin Wright, on the other hand, has been a lot quieter on the event than Garry, happier to remain in the shadows and keep his experience private. According to Garry, the hypnotist, and several others involved in the investigation though, Colin's hypnotic retelling of the lost time matched Garry's up until the point they were separated.

After they were split up onboard the craft, Colin found himself naked in a large perspex-like chamber, bound by the wrists and ankles. He said there were many other chambers in the room, with more people in them. He, too, remembered having some sort of red hot poker inserted into his eye, and feeling as if his brain was swelling. He asked one of the smaller Grey aliens what they wanted with him. The small Grey replied, quite hurtfully, with "It's Garry we want!" It appeared that maybe Garry's abduction had been planned, and that Colin was just taken along for the ride when they unexpectedly found him in the car too. Colin also recounted being taken out of the chamber and dressed by what he called "the wee aliens". He was then back in the car with Garry.

Both men left their encounter with strange scars that they did not have before that night.

Hypnotic regression therapy has been a very controversial investigation technique in ufology. Some say it's very easy to "plant" memories using leading questions and subtle suggestions to have the subject give the responses the hypnotist wants. Others say it could be harmful to the subject's psyche by dragging out hidden, repressed, and painful memories.

Garry disagrees however and is glad he underwent hypnosis to find out what happened on the A70 that night. He claimed that the sessions helped him understand what happened, and though it was quite terrifying, that he was in no danger and they meant him no harm. Outside of the medical experiments, of course.

After learning of his abduction, Garry Wood took up UFO research and became convinced of the presence of extraterrestrial intelligences in the skies over Scotland. He also believes that the government knows about this, and is keeping it under wraps for their own interests. A classified document released by the British government in 2012 revealed that the Ministry of Defence took the mens' abduction *very* seriously.

Abducted, But Why?

The A70 abduction shares many similarities with other famous abduction cases such as Betty & Barney Hill, Travis Walton, and Whitley Strieber. They all feature periods of missing time in the abductees' memories, strange medical experiments being performed on board a spacecraft, and alien beings of similar, if not exact, descriptions — tall, thin, gangly, pale with large heads and eyes, along with smaller counterparts (the brown ones are a little more unique).

Seeing as Garry and Colin reported seeing other human passengers in their unplanned visit to the UFO, could these cases, and many others, be connected? And what happened to the other abductees seen in this craft? Were they too returned with a gap of memory missing, still to this day unsure of what happened?

And what did the aliens want with this pair (or with Garry at least, if he was the one they were after)? What were the experiments in aid of? Surely after all these years of reported abductions, extraterrestrials know what humans are and how we work. Rather than the experiments being for sheer research — which the aliens likely already have in abundance — what if they were trying to extract something from the subjects? What if the aliens were harvesting DNA, bone marrow, stem cells, plasma, and whatever else they needed to work on an alien/human hybrid race? This theory has been put forth for many years as an explanation for alien abduction and experiments and would certainly explain the continued experiments that are still reported to this day.

And what of the tall alien leaders claims that they have always been here? Is this evidence that UFOs and extraterrestrials have been visiting Earth for years? Perhaps even before humans walked the Earth? Does this suggest the possibility that aliens had a hand in the evolution of mankind? If they are indeed harvesting materials from humans to create some sort of new race, perhaps this was done before. Perhaps this is where humans came from originally.

Interestingly just North of Tarbrax, and east of the A70 itself, is Livingston and The Falkirk Triangle. You can draw a straight line from Tarbrax to Dechmont Law, as the crow (or UFO) flies.

The Monster of Glamis

Would it really be a collection of unexplained Scottish mysteries if we didn't visit a castle at least once? Glamis, not content with being known as one of the most haunted castles in the world, also has a more physical, sinister, and rather depressing mystery.

Glamis, a castle in Angus, is said to house a terrible secret. A secret never truly revealed to the public, but kept by the Earls of the castle and passed down from generation to generation.

Birth of A Monster

In the 1840s a rumour began that Glamis Castle had an anonymous guest staying within its walls. Although 'guest' may be too polite of a term - more of a captive. This captive was kept in a secret room somewhere in the castle. But this prisoner was no political prisoner or prisoner of war. In fact, he was allowed out of his secret room to wander the castle at night, travelling through an equally secret passageway, or series of them.

So who was this person kept secret and locked away from public eyes in an unknown room during the day, but allowed to skulk the shadowy castle walls by night?

Lord Glamis, the Earl of Strathmore, married Charlotte Grimstead in 1820. In 1821, their first son was born; the heir to Glamis. Tragically, this son was both born and died on the 18th of October. Or so official records state. What if this son didn't die, but instead survived well into adulthood? What if his death was faked and his existence hidden?

In the coming years, somehow word started to circulate around high society that the son of the Earl had survived, but was born so horribly and disturbingly deformed that he could not be allowed to inherit anything, from titles to castles. So twisted and terrifying was this creature said to be, that not only had his death to be faked to keep him from any inheritance, he also had to be hidden away from human eyes forever. Whether this was to keep up the ruse of the child being dead, to save the family from embarrassment, or if he was truly too horrible to gaze upon is up for debate; though it may be all three.

What makes this story even more tragic however, it was also rumoured that although the child was terribly deformed physically, mentally he was fine. Just a normal person.

As the years went on, and this child would have grown into a teenager and even an adult, the rumours of some humanoid creature hidden away in the castle continued to fly wildly. It wasn't long before people started reporting seeing a strange figure on the battlements of the castle in the dead of night.

Many of these sightings were in an area interestingly known as "The Mad Earl's Walk". While many of these sightings were likely made up, or simply willed into existence due to the rumours, some definitely are believable.

The Adult Monster

In 1865 a workman in the castle saw something very odd. This workman, it is said, came across an unusual door in the course of his employment at the castle. He decided to look inside this door, either out of curiosity or to make sure it wouldn't interfere with his work. The door opened into a long, dark passageway. As horror movies had yet to be invented, he decided it was a totally safe and good idea to go inside for a look.

As he slowly headed down this narrow passageway that seemed to exist inside the walls of the castle itself, he finally saw the end of the passage... At the other end, the workman saw something. It was dark, and the shape he saw was definitely not human, but it was alive. Terrified, the man fled the hidden passageway.

The man reported what he had seen to the Earl. The Earl became uncomfortable and worried. He asked the man if he'd ever thought about moving to Australia. He then told the man he was going to be moving him to Australia. The Earl paid for the man's emigration. Luckily the man agreed to go without argument, who knows how far the Earl would have gone to have kept the workman quiet about his encounter with The Monster of Glamis.

But what exactly did the workman see? It was too dark for him to make out anything definitive. Some snippets of description of the monster did leak out over the years, from apparent witnesses. He was described as having a huge chest and small stumpy limbs, a head with no neck, and being entirely covered in thick hair. He's also been described as a "human toad". If the Loveland Frog Man is anything to go by, that doesn't sound too bad.

Search For The Monster

If this ToadMan did exist, then where is his secret room and passageway? And why has no one found it to this day?

Secret rooms and tunnels in castles aren't unheard of. Castles were built during dangerous times and it was never known when having a nice, secret room to run and hide in would come in handy. Some claim there is a trapdoor at the base of one of the towers along the battlements. This would make it easy for the monster to get to The Mad Earl's Walk, where he had been sighted. Others say there is a trapdoor somewhere in the chapel.

A doctor, while staying at Glamis, reportedly found a trapdoor under the carpet in his room. The trapdoor led to a passageway that ended in a wall that looked far newer than the walls around it. It looked like whatever had been at the end of this passageway had been bricked up. These don't match up to the workmans story though, where he clearly described finding a doorway.

This does not not disprove any of the stories or claims, however. It is not only possible, but very likely, that Glamis has a number of hidden hatches, trapdoors, passageways, and tunnels. Most, perhaps all, will have been there since the castle was built. Long before the need to hide a monster. However, suddenly they had a permanent resident that had to be kept secret and unseen, these secret places around the castle would have taken on a new life. Instead of being used to hide from and escape from attack, they would have been used to traverse the castle in secret.

Some have tried to go right to the source, and find the monster's hidden room.

In 1850, the wife of the 12th Earl asked her friends to help her with a project while her husband was away. The wife, having heard of The Monster of Glamis and sick of her husband giving her no information on the rumour, decided to find out the truth for herself. She thought that if there was a secret room, then it probably had a window. If she could find the window, then perhaps she could locate the room.

She asked all her friends to go to every room in the castle, open every window they could find, and hang a towel out of it. After some time opening countless windows, they all met outside, in the grounds of the castle. Hundreds of windows were open with towels flapping in the breeze. Apart from one that remained tightly shut and toweless.

Before the wife and gang could try and locate the room with the shut window, the 12th Earl unexpectedly returned. The Earl was furious with his wife and her snooping. He swiftly divorced her. Seems like an overreaction, unless she was close to uncovering some terrible secret?

Word Gets Out

How did the rumours of this monster start in the first place?

The secret was so well kept that it was said that the information regarding it was only passed down from an Earl of Glamis to their son on their 21st birthday. Certain members of the royal family were apparently informed, as they kept tabs on all high society in the country. It seems unlikely the royals would gossip about this though, as they would have been far too busy trying to keep their own secrets.

It is thought that a midwife who helped deliver the child knew that he had survived, perhaps she could have spread the word? Her story would have been backed up by the fact that the child had no known grave or headstone.

Some have speculated that after the workman found the strange passageway, a lawyer of the Earl was let into the secret so he could understand why the man was being moved to Australia. Could he have spread the word, intentionally or not?

Was the monster real, or just a rumour that began for pure entertainment? The only way to prove for certain would have been if someone from the time, who would have been told the Glamis secret, spoke publicly about it. This never happened, but some descendents have mentioned it.

An aunt of Elizabeth II who was born in the castle was once asked if she knew anything about the monster. She replied very seriously that her parents forbade her from talking about it when she was a child. She claims she was told to never again ask any questions about the monster. She went on to say that her father and grandfather absolutely refused to talk about it ever, for any reason.

The Monster Is Lost

The secret seems to have been lost, and has never been revealed to more recent Earls. Some say the secret passed from knowledge when an Earl refused to be told it. If he was never told, he could not pass it on. Others say that the secret died with an Earl that perished during the first world war, before he had the chance to tell his heir. No matter where or how the secret died, it seems needless to have continued passing it down for so long after the monster would have died from natural causes anyway.

Now it seems the only way to prove there was ever a monster in Glamis would be to find some sort of family record of it. A record that likely would never have existed, given how secret they wanted to keep him.

There may be a way to definitively prove there once existed a monster inside Glamis Castle. If someone were to find one of the hidden trap doors or entrances to a secret passageway and follow it, they might just find a room that no one has been in for over a hundred years. If they could find evidence that this room had been lived in, perhaps then we could confidently say that a poor deformed child, stripped of his title of

Earl and forced to live his life in secret, was indeed kept inside this castle.

And who's to say The Monster of Glamis doesn't still exist inside the castle in some form? After such a tortured life, would it be any wonder if his spirit had joined the legion of ghosts said to already inhabit Glamis? Perhaps late at night, a shadowy figure that looks not quite human can still be seen skulking The Mad Earl's Walk.

The Bargarran
Possession

Demonic possession — we've all heard of it and seen it in some sort of media. Most of us are likely familiar with it because of *The Exorcist*, a film in which a young girl spews green soup and makes libellous comments about people's mothers, but the idea of possession has appeared in far more than just one movie. It has appeared on the big screen countless times, has been the basis for TV shows, video games, comic books, novels, and more. But where did this idea of demonic possession come from? Was it just a good idea dreamed up by entertainment industry creatives?

Far from it. Humans being possessed by supernatural forces have been reported for years and continue to this day. It's been openly acknowledged by the church, and many religious people believe that evil forces can indeed enter the body of a person and force them to do strange and terrible things.

Many classic cases of possession can now be explained as undiagnosed mental illness that sadly resulted in brutal exorcisms; more akin to torture than any real help, that caused great harm and even death to those that were subjected to them. However some cases stand apart and seem to be unexplainable unless one considers the paranormal.

In 1697, the 11 year old daughter of the Laird of Bargarran experienced a case of demonic possession that could have come straight out of a horror movie, complete with contortion, horrific vomiting, and the Devil himself.

Possession Begins

It began on the night of the 21st of August when Christian, the daughter of John Shaw, had her first experience that suggested something unusual may be happening to her. She suddenly woke from a deep sleep, screamed, levitated, and flew across the room. Her father heard the noise, ran to her room, and found Christian laying on the floor, as stiff as if she were dead. It took her days to recover, and even after she did, she complained of still being in pain, but with no obvious cause.

Soon after this, her body started to contort against her will. Her limbs would bend at impossible angles without her consciously moving them. In one instance, her body bent so far backwards that her head and her feet touched the floor at the same time. As abnormal as this was, Christian had an idea of what may be causing her bizarre involuntary behaviour.

A few days earlier Christian had seen one of the family servants, Catherine Campbell, steal a glass of milk. She told her mother about what she saw, and Catherine was swiftly fired for such an egregious breach of contract. Catherine cursed Christian, reportedly saying she wished the Devil would drag her soul through Hell. Snitches get stitches.

Christian soon claimed that during the night she was being visited by Catherine Campbell and Agnes Naismith; a woman suspected of being a witch who had spoken to Christian the day before she had her first paranormal episode.

These women would appear in her room and stab Christian while she lay in bed. Catherine and Agnes were totally invisible to everyone except for Christian. The knives they would stab her with left no marks, but certainly inflicted physical pain on her. She would writhe in her bed from the agony these invisible women would inflict upon her. She attempted to speak to her tormentors multiple times to find out why they were torturing her, but she got no answer. As if being stabbed wasn't bad enough, she was also getting the silent treatment!

One night the two women didn't turn up. In their place, she was visited by the Devil. Satan must have been having a slow night, because he seemingly turned up just to argue with Christian. He heckled and annoyed her for hours, while she endlessly quoted Bible verses to try and scare him off.

A Rational Explanation

Despite everything that was happening to his daughter, John Shaw believed it was something perfectly normal that doctors could diagnose. Many doctors tried and failed to treat her, as her condition continued to worsen.

At the three month mark, John and Christian travelled by boat up the Clyde River in Glasgow to get to their appointment with the best doctor they could find. During the journey, Christian fell even more ill. She began to vomit up long strands of hair that varied in colour, shocking the other passengers and putting them off their dinner.

When John and Christian arrived at their destination, Doctor Andrew Brisbane began his examination. It wasn't long into her check up before she was struck by the urge to vomit again. This time what spewed from her mouth was even stranger than the technicoloured hair. She chucked up hot coals that landed sizzling on the ground. Brisbane tried to pick up the coals, but found them too hot to handle. Christian was then sent home no closer to a cure for her "illness".

Back at Bargarran House, Christian spent the next few days continuing her vast vomiting spree. She brought up bones, straw, eggshells, pins, and other oddities; the worst of which has to be animal dung (this also likely gave her bad breath). During a second appointment with Dr. Brisbane, Christian got a bird bone stuck in her throat while heaving it up. An assistant to the good doctor jammed his hand in her mouth to try and pry it out, but was shocked when he felt another force trying to pull it back down. It felt as if another hand was reaching out from inside Christian and playing tug of war with the bone.

One night in late December, while once again under attack by the invisible witches, Christian managed to grab one. A tear was heard, and in Christians hand was a scrap of fabric that she hadn't been holding prior. It seemed as if she had grabbed hold of one of the witches, and in their attempt to escape her clutch, a part of their cloak had ripped off and become visible.

Catching The Culprits

At this point, John Shaw considered the possibility that his daughter's illness might be outside the realms of normality. He thought the most logical reason behind his daughters otherworldly torture was witchcraft.

In January 1698, a literal witch hunt began to try and find those responsible for Christian's curse. Several men and women, including Catherine Campbell and Agnes Naismith, were arrested under suspicion of practising the dark arts.

After some creative interrogation techniques involving sharp objects, many of them confessed to having made an unholy pact with the Devil. In June of that same year, seven of the accused were hanged and their bodies burned. As she died, Agnes Naismith cast a curse on everyone involved in her trial and execution. Catherine Campbell made a similar threat as she was carried to the gallows, reportedly calling down the wrath of the Devil on everyone present. One witness to the executions claimed that as the bodies burned, some came back to life and their limbs attempted to crawl out of the fire.

After the executions, Christian seemed to totally recover. She never again experienced any strange paranormal events. She later married the Reverend John Millar in 1719, who died two years afterward. Following his death, Christian went on to produce the Bargarran Thread, a hugely popular thread that made her rich and was instrumental in shaping the town of Paisley.

She was married a second time in 1737, and passed away that same year. Her grave can be found in Greyfriars Kirk in Edinburgh; interestingly one of the most haunted graveyards in the world.

Was She Truly Possessed?

Was Christian truly cursed by witches and possessed by demons? Some have suggested that the mere threat of a curse from Catherine Campbell may have thrown Christian into an extended fit of hysteria. This could have caused seizures, which might explain her strange contortions and how she seemingly flew across a room. It doesn't explain her revolting regurgitations however.

Some believe Christian faked the whole thing. Sceptics have said that Christian was simply a good contortionist and had full control of her body, and only acted as if an otherworldly presence was bending her. This was backed up in 1839 when a small hole was found hidden in the wall of Christian's old bedroom. It is believed that she could have been passed objects through this hole by a co-conspirator or hidden items inside of it — perhaps even the same inexplicable items she claimed to have vomited up. It's a reasonable explanation, but it doesn't explain the things people personally saw her throw up, like the hot coals.

Despite some believable attempts to debunk Christain's apparent possession, no one has been able to disprove and explain everything that happened. The only other possibility is the story has become exaggerated over time. Could so much have been embellished in the years between? Or could Christian truly have been possessed by dark forces?

And did they leave after the witches were executed? Or did the demonic forces just settle down a bit and lay low, trying to not draw attention to themselves? Could the Bargarran thread actually have been the creation of these demons? And when the thread is used, could this actually be the performance of a dark occult ritual without the tailor even knowing?

Unlikely, but the next time you use the Bargarran thread just be careful you aren't sewing yourself a portal to Hell.

Morag: The Monster of Loch Morar

We all know Nessie, the monster of Loch Ness, but what about her less popular cousin; Morag?

Morag is a monster said to inhabit Loch Morar in Lochaber, located in the Highlands of Scotland. While she may not be as widely known, talked about, or tourist friendly, she is far more likely to exist than her more famous cousin. So why do we know so little of Morag? Why is she forever cursed to play second fiddle to Nessie? Why is she The Damned to Nessie's Sex Pistols?

Loch Morar & The Monster Appears

Unlike Loch Ness, Loch Morar is much more difficult to get to —and when you do get there, there is not even a proper walking trail around the entire loch. Because of this, there are no hordes of people disturbing the loch and its surroundings, making a peaceful environment for a creature to live.

Along with the relative peacefulness of Loch Morar making it a great place for a cryptid to reside, it is also one of the deepest inland lochs not just in Scotland, but in Europe. It reaches depths of over one thousand feet, and is eleven miles long and one and a half miles wide.

Even with the large size of Loch Morar and its difficulty to reach, sightings of a creature in its waters have been constant. The first sighting of Morag was likely in the 19th century, though it could have been even earlier.

In these early reports, Morag is described as something like a mermaid: a creature with the bottom half of a fish, the upper half of a woman, with a head of long golden hair. In these sightings, seeing Morag was considered a death omen; much like hearing a banshee.

From the 20th century onwards Morag took on a look that was more like her cousin, described as a creature with three humps and a snake-like head poking out of the water. It was only after the 1930's that more significant and frequent sightings of Morag were reported. This was perhaps due to more people being in the area of Loch Morar and catching a glimpse of her, or possibly because of Nessies sudden rise of popularity around this time, she decided her cousin couldn't have all the fun.

Morag Strikes

On August 16, 1969, William Simpson and Duncan McDonald were casually sailing on the loch in a motorboat. As they cruised along, both men suddenly heard splashing behind them. The splashing was too loud and heavy to be caused by the boat or any known fish in the loch. The men made their way to the back of the boat and were shocked to see a large object speeding towards their vessel, cutting through their wake.

It took the creature only seconds to catch up with the boat, and then collided with it. The men were sure this collision was an intentional attack. They were also sure they had been struck by a creature of some kind, and not just some piece of massive driftwood with a vendetta.

The collision stopped the creature, and it seemed to tread water in place. It was during this time that the men managed to get a better look at what had hit their boat. They saw an animal that they estimated to be 25 to 30 feet in length. The creature's skin looked rough and was a dark brown. They could see three humps emerging from the water, along with a serpentine head.

The men were worried that this monster was recomposing itself, shaking off a possible concussion, to dive under their boat and try to capsize it. Luckily Simpson had his shotgun handy and blasted a shot into the water beside the creature. Whether or not he was actually aiming at Morag or was just a bad shot is unknown. Either way, the shot scared the creature and it disappeared back into the depths of the loch.

A year later, in September 1970, a creature of the same description was seen by Charles Fishburne. He described seeing a large dark humped creature swimming quickly through the loch.

In 1990 a similar encounter to Simpson and Duncan's took place. On the 18th of August, Alistair McKellaig, his brother, and his two sons were fishing from a boat on the loch. While they were fishing, McKellaig spotted three humped objects about 50 yards behind the boat. He said each hump stood three feet out of the water and reminded him of tyres. The objects were clearly moving and keeping pace with the boat. Luckily for these anglers, Morag didn't ram the boat like she did in 1969. Maybe she learned her lesson after being shot at.

She simply overtook the boat and disappeared back into the deep waters. McKellaig was a frequent fisher on the loch and was familiar with it and its surroundings, so it's unlikely he would have seen something natural and confused it for a monster.

In 2013, Doug and Charlotte Christie were holidaying at a B&B near the loch. They claim to have spotted Morag three times during their two day stay.

They described seeing a 20 foot long dark object in the loch, with humps poking out of the water. Initially they thought the humps were just rocks, until they realised the object was moving. Plus, the water was also far too deep for rocks to break the surface.

Some have even claimed to have seen Morag on the shores of the loch. Some have said they have found animal footprints along the shore that they could not match to any known creature in the area.

In 1996, a diver in the loch found a pile of bones in the depths of Morar. Many were curious as to whether this would prove to be the skeleton of Morag herself. After some research however, these bones turned out to belong to a deer. This contributed to the theory that Morag could move both in and out of the water. Some theorised that Morag would leave the loch to hunt, dragging her prey back to the murky depths to feed.

Is She A Monster?

What is Morag? What is the creature that lurks in Loch Morar? Is it an undiscovered creature? Something that has survived from ancient times, while other members of its species have gone extinct?

There have been few attempts to find Morag, save for an expedition by monster hunter Adrian Shine. In 1975, he began searching the depths of the loch in a homemade submersible. Sounds perfectly safe. He sadly found no evidence despite his vast research. He has since moved on to searching for Nessie. He founded The Loch Ness Project and has worked tirelessly to find proof of this monster. He is a true hero of cryptozoology.

There is a theory that Morag and Nessie are actually the same creature. Some have theorised that a vast system of underwater tunnels connect Loch Morar to Loch Ness, and possibly even to other locations in the country.

Could it be possible that one creature travels between the two lochs? It would explain why Nessie and Morag have never been seen at the same time. It would also explain where the creature could be during its long downtimes between sightings. It could be in an entirely different place in Scotland, with no witnesses to see it.

Is it possible Morag is something more supernatural? Psychics who have visited the loch have said that the area is alive with mystic energy. Could Loch Morar be in a location where the veil between this world and some parallel dimension is thin? Could Morag be a creature from another world who occasionally slips through into ours? It would explain its seemingly endless lifespan, its elusiveness and its otherworldly appearance. It's a theory that has also been put forth to explain other mysterious cryptids such as Bigfoot, The Jersey Devil, The Fresno Nightcrawlers, and more.

Is it also a coincidence that sightings of Nessie and Morag both increased in the years following a certain occultist's demonic ritual on the shores of Loch Ness?

Could Crowley, while attempting to perform his Abremelin ritual, have inadvertently ripped open the veil even wider, allowing Nessie more freedom in this world where she used the subterranean tunnels between lochs to travel? Could it have been freed from whatever prison Saint Columba trapped it in? It would explain why Morag suddenly went from looking like a mermaid to a prehistoric sea serpent. Perhaps the mermaid was an entirely different creature, while Morag/Nessie was just given the same name.

Whether Morag is a physical beast travelling through underwater tunnels, a spiritual creature travelling through dimensional holes ripped by Crowley (or something in between), whether or not she is the same cryptid as Nessie, or an entirely different monster, there is certainly something strange dwelling in both lochs. Something that shows no sign of going away.

The Calvine UFO Photo

Why are UFO pictures always so blurry?

It seems like whenever a new photo of an alleged alien craft makes its way to our eyes, it's always out of focus and hard to tell what we're actually looking at. Even in today's world of HD cameras built into mobile phones that most of the population are carrying at any given moment, it seems like no one can snap a convincing photo of extraterrestrial craft.

Many looking for definitive proof of visitors to Earth from another planet ask "Has there ever been a clear photograph of a UFO? A photo that even the most sceptical of people could not doubt?" Many have theorised that such images do exist, but are never allowed to be seen by anyone other than those who took them and the people in the government agencies who confiscate them and lock them away. This may sound like the far-fetched ravings of a basement dwelling, tin foil hat wearing, conspiracy theorist, but it could in fact be exactly what happened to two anonymous hillwalkers in the early 90's.

The Pictures

In August of 1990 two hillwalkers, believed to be local chefs, were out hiking in Calvine, near Perthshire. While enjoying the scenery they suddenly saw something very unusual in the sky. They saw an unidentified flying object hovering silently over the landscape. The craft was a diamond shape, and they estimated it to be around 100 feet long. The men were so shocked by what they were seeing that they instinctively hid in some nearby bushes. One of the hikers, thinking fast, pointed his camera out of their leafy hiding place and started snapping photos of the bizarre rhombus shaped object.

In the ten minutes the hikers observed the UFO, they said they saw military jets passing by, circling and observing the object, at least one of which is seen in the photos taken. Soon after taking the final photo, the craft took off at speed, perhaps being pursued by one of the jets. In total, the hiker took six photographs of the UFO.

The hikers got their photos developed as soon as they could. This being the early nineties, and having no access to a darkroom, meant taking them to a pharmacy and waiting a few days to get them back. Once getting their negatives returned, and being sure they had definitely captured images of something very out of the ordinary (and perhaps out of this world), they thought about what they should do with them.

They decided that the public should see these photos, and sent the six negatives to a newspaper; The Daily Record. The Daily Record were amazed by the pictures and were working on an article to print along with them. In order to get as much information as possible, and to make sure they weren't faked, they sent the negatives, some prints they had made of the photos, and several questions to the Ministry of Defence. They were never returned.

The Ministry of Defence kept the photos and also never disclosed the identities of the hikers who saw the craft. In late 2020 the pictures were expected to finally be released by the MoD under the thirty year rule, which says that certain classified documents will be released to the public thirty years after they are created. An unknown person decided to extend the closure of the Calvine UFO case by fifty years, meaning the photos could not be released to the public until 2070.

Or at least, they couldn't be released *officially*.

The Search

An investigative journalist named David Clarke became interested in the missing photos, and sought to track them down. He began by trying to find either of the two witnesses to the craft.

While he was not able to find either witness, he was able to find the next best thing. He tracked down a retired RAF Press Officer who had received a print that The Daily Record had sent to the MoD when trying to confirm their validity.

Clarke contacted the Press Officer in August of 2021, just over a year since the photos were locked up for a further half a century. Reportedly the man said "I've been waiting more than thirty years for someone to call me about this." The retired man explained how he had been sent a picture and details of one of the witnesses. He had interviewed the witness, written out a report, made a copy of the photo, and mailed it all to his superiors in the Ministry of Defence... then heard nothing else.

After several phone interviews where Clarke asked the man about the photo and the details surrounding him receiving it, Clarke travelled to meet him in May of 2022. Here Clarke found what he had been searching for. The former Press Officer still had in his possession, in its original envelope, the picture sent to him by The Daily Record.

As Clarke saw the elusive photo, being perhaps the first new person to gaze upon it for 32 years, he naturally asked if he could make a copy of it. The retired man was happy to let Clarke photograph it, but his only condition was that he not handle it or reveal the name written on the back of the photograph, which was believed to be the name of the original hiking photographer; a very fair request so as to not intrude on anyone's privacy.

Clarke agreed and he photographed the photograph while it was being held by the Press Officer against a piece of cardboard to totally eliminate the chance of the name on the back being revealed.

The Calvine UFO photo turned out to be everything many ufologists hoped it would be. It did indeed show a diamond shaped object in a cloudy sky, with an aircraft just below it. At the bottom of the frame is the top of a fence and at the top left are some branches. It is one of the clearest and most convincing pictures of an Unidentified Flying Object ever shared with the public.

In June of 2022 Clarke met with the retired man once again, and he donated the picture and his report to Sheffield Hallam Universities

Special Collection. Now high quality scans were able to be done on the photograph and shared with the world.

Along with a better look at the image, the name on the back was revealed: Kevin Russell. Clarke began a search for the man, but it proved futile. A man by that name was believed to have worked in a hotel near Calvine in 1990, but all attempts to track him down have so far been in vain.

What's Really In The Pictures?

Why were these pictures locked up by the MOD initially? Did the hikers really see a craft from another world? Some have said they saw an experimental military aircraft, and that is why the images were confiscated and hidden initially, but surely a thirty year old piece of military hardware is no longer worth concealing from the public.

Who made the decision to block the release of the Calvine photos in 2020, and why? What did these hikers capture on camera that is too shocking for the public to see for at least eighty years? It's hard to imagine they saw something mundane.

And if we remember, the hikers took six photos. We've only seen one. What happened to the other five? What happened to the negatives that were sent to the newspaper? It seems that the Press Officer was only sent one printed photograph, and no negatives.

Could it be that there was only one photo, and the amount has been exaggerated over time? Or could The Daily Record have kept a hold of the other five negatives? Could they possibly have only sent the MoD one? Could the newspaper have destroyed them, or just lost them, in some time over the last thirty plus years?

Or were all six kept by the MoD after they received them, locked away forever in some giant secret warehouse along with debris from the Roswell crash and The Ark of the Covenant? Or, when word of the images reached them, did the Men in Black step in, confiscate all the prints and negatives, and put a stop to the entire investigation? It could explain why The Daily Record never ran a story on the original pictures, or their mysterious disappearance. It could also explain why the photos were not planned to be seen by the public for another 50 years (at least!).

Or could it possibly be that *no original negatives were sent*? Could Kevin Russell have kept a hold of the originals, and only sent a copy to the newspaper? Could the negatives, and all the original six images, still be in the possession of this man to this day, wherever he may now be?

If there is a lesson to be learned from this story, it's if you manage to get a photo of a UFO, or indeed anything paranormal or supernatural, always hold on to a copy. And who knows, maybe one of these hikers did make copies that he or she has kept hidden and secret for over thirty years. Copies that they may soon be convinced to release (If you're reading this: come on, you know you want to!)

Robert Gordon & The Devil

Is Satan real? And if he is, can you make a deal with him in exchange for your soul?

It's a question that seems to have existed since tempus immemorial (that means forever). Tales of people selling their immortal souls to the devil in exchange for wealth, talent, and success are far from unheard of, and have been attached to everyone from business tycoons, painters, composers, inventors, rock stars, and everything in between. But has anyone actually ever sold their souls to the big man himself, or are these tales simply born out of jealousy over others' success? Often, people think that these people could not have possibly made it on their own.

If you could sell your soul, what would you ask for? And what would you do when the devil came calling?

Robert Sells His Soul

Sir Robert Gordon was born in 1647 and was the 3rd Baronet of Gordonstoun in Elgin. Due to his place in high society and his reputation as a brilliant student, he was able to travel to Italy to complete his higher studies as a teenager.

During his time in Italy he became obsessed with maths and science. He became so knowledgeable in these subjects that many began to believe that he couldn't have simply learned through books and teaching. People began to speculate that the only way Robert could have become so clever was by selling his soul to the devil in exchange for vast knowledge.

When Robert returned to Gordonstoun, the rumours followed him home. These rumours said that in exchange for his new understanding of the sciences, the devil would return for his soul in thirty years.

Because of these rumours, his extensive knowledge, and his eccentricities, people began to refer to him as The Wizard of Gordonstoun, even though his actual magical powers were more rooted in science. He was certainly no Wizard of Yester.

Robert had a round house constructed that was connected to nearby sea caves by a secret tunnel. It was in this round abode that Robert conducted his scientific experiments. It was also in this circular building that locals claimed to see Robert dancing naked with women. This just seems like a fun party, but locals also reported seeing more sinister activities. They claimed to have seen him drinking and playing cards with Satan himself. Perhaps he was trying to win his soul back?

Around this time, the community flooded the rumour mill once again. Reportedly, Robert cast no shadow and he was slowly roasting a salamander (which I sincerely hope is not a euphemism) over the course of seven years for reasons no one could really explain. Some have theorised this was part of a ritual to attempt to free himself of his deal with the devil. A ritual that did not quite work out.

Time To Pay The Devil

The years went on, and soon enough it was time for Robert to pay the devil. The night before the payment was due, Satan paid him a polite visit and let him know he'd be returning at midnight the next evening to collect what he was owed.

In a panic the next morning, Robert called for a priest. He asked the priest to sit with him through the night to ward off the devil. It was during this time that Robert told the priest the reason for why he had his house built round. It was so the devil would be unable to corner him. It seemed he planned to just run in circles until the devil got tired of chasing him and gave up (I mean, that's my plan).

As the sun set, a terrible storm began. As midnight drew closer and closer, the priest was overcome with fear and fled the round house. Before leaving he told Robert the only way to save his soul was to head to holy grounds. The closest holy ground was twenty miles away: Birnie Kirk.

Robert leaped on his horse and started galloping towards the kirk. Soon he heard the sound of hooves behind him. Robert glanced back and saw the devil chasing him on his black steed. He then heard the sounds of growling, snarling and barking; the hounds of hell were also on his heels.

Birnie Kirk was in sight and Robert spurred his horse onwards. A hellhound leaped at his horse, and sunk its teeth into its backside. The horse bucked, throwing Robert off and over its head. Robert landed on the frozen ground head first, breaking his neck and killing him. As he hit the ground, the clock struck midnight.

The hellhounds devoured his horse, and the devil approached to claim Robert's soul. The devil stopped short of Robert's body. When the horse threw him off, Robert had landed just inside the grounds of Birnie Kirk. He made it to holy ground. The Devil was unable to claim his soul, forced to return to hell empty handed and slightly annoyed.

In the morning, Robert's body was discovered and taken to the local undertakers. The next night, his body mysteriously disappeared and a coffin full of bricks was buried in its place, or so the legend goes.
It is said that ever since no black horse has, or can, enter the grounds of Birnie Kirk..

Could Robert have sold his soul to the devil in exchange for vast scientific knowledge? Selling one's soul in exchange for unholy talent is a fairly common tale, though most people choose to be able to shred on guitar rather than increase their mathematical skills. With his newly obtained knowledge, Robert was able to create a better sea pump (a machine used to circulate seawater on board a ship) that was used by the navy. It's not a classic rock album, but it's something.

And what about Robert's body? After it was removed from the holy ground, did the Devil send his minions to collect it, or come for it himself? Maybe he found some fine print in the contract that said his soul was only safe as long as the body remained in a sacred site, on holy ground?

If you should choose to perform a dark ritual to sell your soul to Satan, make sure you read that contract thoroughly. Don't just click accept like it's an online terms and conditions.

Edinburgh's Tiny Coffins

One of the best things about going for a nice country walk in Scotland is that there's always something new to find or see. Maybe you'll spot a type of bird you've never seen before, or stumble across an old croft, or find a path that used to be a railway line. All very wholesome, but not every discovery in the nature of Scotland is a pleasant one.

A Disturbing Discovery

In 1836 a group of school boys made their way up Arthur's Seat, an extinct volcano and the highest peak of a group of hills just outside Edinburgh. The boys had made this trip in hope of seeing some rabbits, but instead stumbled across something far more sinister.

As they ascended Arthur's Seat one of the boys spotted something that grabbed his attention. What he saw was three pieces of slate, something that looked quite out of place on a hillside. This was before the time of Pokemon and Nintendo, so kids still found this kind of thing interesting. He pointed it out to his friends, and they went over to investigate. When they picked up the slates, they realised they were covering a small hole in the ground. But this wasn't some ordinary hole, dug by the much sought after rabbits, but a tiny mass grave.

In the hole were 17 miniature coffins, each only 95mm long. Inside each coffin was a tiny, hand carved person dressed in an individual outfit. The kids were alarmed and fascinated by this find and quickly shared it. All these years later, the same questions remain: Who made these coffins, who put them here, and why?

Why Arthur's Seat?

Could the location of Arthur's Seat have any relevance, or was it simply a good hiding place?

Arthur's Seat has a history of strange tales and legends. Many have said it is a possible site for King Arthur's Camelot, that an apostle once climbed Arthur's Seat and claimed he spoke to god at the top, some women believed it housed the fountain of youth, it has a generally bloody history, and is thought to still be a site of Pagan and occult rituals to this day.

Could the coffins have been placed here as part of some sort of elaborate occult ritual? Could someone have been trying to contact God himself with these tiny offerings? Were they attempting to conjure the fountain of youth? Was it left as an offering to King Arthur, Merlin and the Knights of the Round Table? All possible, but seemingly unlikely.

Perhaps the answer lies in what the purpose of the coffins and the tiny figures inside was. One possible explanation put forward to explain the coffins is witchcraft.

Some think the human figures inside the coffins were some sort of voodoo doll. Voodoo dolls are generally made in the likeness of a person, and made from an easily destructible material like wax. The idea, as I'm sure you've seen in countless pieces of media and even previously in this book during the tale of The Glasgow Witches, is to damage or destroy this effigy and have the damage magically transfer to the person it is based on.

The figures in the coffins didn't appear to be in the likeness of anyone in particular though, and were made from strong wood. The coffins also seemed to protect the figures from the weather and environment by design. Even the slates placed on the hole they were buried in seemed to be as much for protection as it was for secrecy. Whoever made these figures wanted them to last and to be kept in good condition. The opposite of what you want from a good voodoo doll.

Another theory is that the coffins are somehow related to a Saxon burial tradition. This involves burying a small model of a person who died far from home. This seems reasonable, but how the tiny coffins play into these burial rites is unknown. It also seems unlikely that so many Saxon's could be living in Edinburgh in the 1800's, a city that was widely Christian.

An interesting theory is that the coffins are somehow connected to Burke & Hare; the infamous body snatchers. Burke and Hare would murder people for the purpose of selling their corpses to science.
Burke and Hare had 17 victims, the same number of coffins that were found. They were also active in Edinburgh in 1828, just eight years before these coffins were discovered. However, 12 of Burke & Hare's victims were female, and it seemed all 17 figures were male. Is it possible someone was trying to recreate the victims of the body snatchers in miniature form, but simply wasn't familiar with female anatomy and did the best they could? This was well before the time of the internet and the millions of reference images of the female form that came with it.

However, we still have no idea who *made* the coffins. Could it have been someone connected to the murders, who was so racked with guilt they decided to make these figures? Or someone who wanted to pay their respect to the victims of Burke & Hare? If so, why hide them on Arthur's Seat? As far as we know, this location holds no significance to the body snatchers' crimes.

The 18th Coffin & More Investigations

In 1990 the tiny coffins and figures were examined in more detail. It was discovered that the figures were carved by hand, probably by a single person, but the coffins themselves may have been built by 2 different people.

The materials used point towards them being made by a shoemaker or something similar. The fabric on the clothes placed on the figures was discovered to have been from the early 1830's, meaning the coffins couldn't have been hidden for more than 6 years.

Could the Edinburgh coffins have been a collaboration project and not the work of a single individual as previously thought?

And then, there is the 18th coffin.

In December 2014 the National Museum of Scotland received an anonymous package. The package was marked XVIII; 18 in Roman numerals. The package contained a new coffin and figure inside, made in exactly the same way and with the same materials as the ones found by the boys in 1836. Inside the package was also a paragraph from the Robert Louis Stevenson poem The Body Snatchers, written in 1884. So, where did this 18th coffin come from?

Could it be a descendant of the original coffin maker who has had the secret passed down to him? Or the original coffin maker himself came back from the dead? Or is the original creator an immortal creature, and simply returned to his work after almost 200 years?

As interesting as this would be, I think it's safe to assume this 18th coffin is something of a homage. Perhaps an artist was inspired by the original coffins and the mystery that surrounded them and decided to make a new one, and even add to the mystery himself.

But what about the original 17 coffins?

It was discovered that the coffins were placed on Arthur's Seat one, two or three at a time. This means that whoever placed them under the slates had made many trips to store the coffins in their resting place. Was 17 the number that whoever was making these coffins intended to stop at? Or was he interrupted in the middle of his project by the children finding them?

If the coffin maker hadn't reached his desired number, perhaps it's possible that he hid future coffins in a new place. Perhaps somewhere in Edinburgh, hidden for almost 200 years, is a secret cache of tiny coffins. If someone were to find this second hiding place, we may be closer to uncovering the answers behind the purpose of the coffins and discovering the identity of who created them.

The Gorbals Vampire

Vampires are usually associated with Transylvania, but over the years they have appeared all over the place: Santa Carla, Sunnydale, and even Glasgow. But what is a vampire?

There's been so many iterations of the creature over the years that it's hard to come up with any definitive image. Are vampires Christopher Lee skulking around a gothic castle? Teenagers with mullets and motorcycle jackets? Well-dressed 17th century fops with unconvincing accents? Are they old and decaying or eternally youthful? Are they allergic to crosses and garlic? Do they burst into flame when touched by sunlight, or do they just sparkle in it?

Even the teeth have gone through many different designs; from the pointy, monstrous maw of Nosferatu to the more subtle fangs of Bela Lugosi. Sometimes the teeth aren't even teeth at all, but rather long iron daggers.

In 1954, hordes of children swarmed the South Necropolis graveyard in the Gorbals of Glasgow armed with whatever they could find. Their goal was to find The Gorbals Vampire, a seven foot tall entity with iron teeth said to live in the graveyard, and to put an end to its reign of terror.

But what was The Gorbals Vampire? How did the children all know about it? And, most importantly, did they find it?

An After School Vampire Hunt

On September 23, 1954 a strange rumour began circulating around the Glasgow schools. The story was that a vampire-like creature with metal teeth had kidnapped two young boys, killed them, drank their blood, and then eaten their flesh. It was said this vampire was living in the South Necropolis — also known as The City Of The Dead (cool name, right?).

No one knows who started this rumour, and the police claim there were no reports of missing children at this time. For the school kids in the area though, this rumour caught their imaginations. It spread from kid to kid in record time, going viral in an age before mobile phones and internet memes.

Almost immediately a plan formed, and it spread as quickly as the vampire rumour. After school, every child would arm themselves. Then they would meet at the Necropolis, find the vampire, and kill it before it could abduct any more children. When the bell sounded, the kids rushed out of school, and got to the graveyard as fast they could. They picked up sticks, knives, bricks, and whatever else they could lay their hands on on their way to the Necropolis. Glasgow kids are very resourceful when it comes to weapons.

Over 200 children — some so young they could barely walk and others in their early teens — stormed the graveyard. They searched every inch of the large Necropolis. There were hundreds of tombstones and mausoleums, as well as large wooded areas. As night began to fall, the graveyard began to take on even more of a horror movie aesthetic. Fog began to roll in, which mixed with the setting sun made visibility difficult and dramatic. Next to the graveyard was a steelworks factory, which erupted fire into the sky, suddenly illuminating the Necropolis in a bright red flash which cast strange shadows from the tombstones, before fading back into darkness. Again and again, these shadows were mistaken for the vampire. A shout would go up, the children would rush over but would find nothing.

Eventually the police turned up to try and find out what was happening. They spoke to whatever children they could drag away from

124

their hunt, and they were told about the vampire. At first the police thought this was some kind of joke or maybe a game the kids were playing. As they continued their investigation, they realised that the kids were deadly serious. The police tried to get everyone to give up the hunt but they would not be dissuaded. The crowd only began to leave when it started to rain. You cannot battle the undead if you're soggy.

The next night, the children continued the hunt, but once again no vampire was found. After the third night, the number of children on the hunt had diminished, but word of the vampire had reached their parents.

The adults were concerned about stories they'd been hearing from their kids. Many contacted the police to ask if there was any truth to the tales of child abduction and cannibalism. Of course, the police reassured them that there was nothing to worry about. Around this time, the story was picked up by the local newspapers. Then the national newspapers. Then the international press. Everyone wanted to know where this story of a vampire had come from, and what had sent this army of vampire slaying children on their graveyard hunt.

What Inspired The Vampire?

The first culprit the media blamed was horror based comic books — 1954 was still far too early for them to start pinning things on heavy metal and Dungeons & Dragons. A 1953 issue of *Dark Mysteries* contained a story called "The Vampire With The Iron Teeth." It isn't hard to make the connection from the vampire in this comic to the description of the Gorbals Vampire.

The only issue with this theory is that Dark Mysteries was an American comic, and there is no evidence to suggest any of these Scottish kids had access to such comics. No child questioned made mention of any comic and no parent ever claimed their offspring had any copies. Whatsmore, most of the pint sized Van Helsings didn't even know what a vampire was.

This was long before vampires had such a huge place in popular culture. All these kids knew was that there was some weird tall creature with metal teeth that had been supposedly killing kids. None of them brought garlic, holy water, stakes, or even a crucifix. Good thing they didn't find the vampire; it would have been a very one sided fight.

So if evil American horror comics didn't warp the young and impressionable minds of these kids, what did?

One answer might be closer to home. In the early 1800s another beast with iron teeth haunted the children of Glasgow. Jenny Wi' (With) The Iron Teeth was a witch-like entity that was said to stalk the park of Glasgow Green. Jenny was never a real creature, rather a story that parents told kids to make them go to sleep. If they didn't get to bed soon, Jenny would come and eat them. Yeah, that would send me right to sleep too.

Could a child in the Gorbals have heard this old story from a parent or grandparent, given it a modern makeover, and accidentally caused a little bit of mass hysteria in the playground?

Whatever caused the hunt for The Gorbals Vampire and whether or not it was actually real, it was certainly a real entity in the minds of several hundred school kids for at least a few days. Perhaps for just a few days The Gorbals Vampire was made into a physical, living creature through the combined collective unconscious psychic ability of these children and their unwavering belief in the impossible?

Perhaps just another few children in the hunt could have given this entity the power to actually attack, abduct, and devour helpless victims. I'm sure I don't have to explain the concept of a tulpa again? Breathe a sigh of relief.

The Brahan Seer

The ability to predict the future through dreams and visions is nothing new. People have claimed to have this ability for as long as others have been willing to believe it. Perhaps the most famous of these people, or "seers" as they are known, is Nostradamus.

Despite living in the 1500s and his predictions being both quite vague and very open to interpretation, people still believe his prophecies are coming true today. Disasters, both natural and man-made, are regularly linked to something Nostradamus scribbled down several hundred years prior. Because of this, he has been the subject of many books, articles, and papers of research. The fascination with Nostradamus continues to this day, and his influence and place in pop culture cannot be overstated. From his predictions and life influencing the plots of movies, novels, and TV shows, he's even appeared in cartoon form and inspired a heavy metal concept album.

Perhaps what made Nostradamus so famous was that his prophecies found relevance across the globe — or could at least be interpreted that way.

Scotland had its own, more local, Nostradamus. The predictions made by The Brahan Seer specifically related to his country and, much like his more famous counterpart, are still thought to be coming true today.

Birth Of A Seer

The story of The Brahan Seer is full of doubt and debate, with some even believing that he never actually existed. Those who do believe in him and his prophecies tend to agree that he was born in the 17th century on the island now known as Lewis. The real name of The Brahan Seer is thought to have been Kenneth Mackenzie, but having developed psychic abilities at a very young age he became known as Coinneach Odhar in Scottish Gaelic, or Dark Kenneth in English. Whether or not there existed a Light Kenneth has been lost to history.

It was said that Dark Kenneth used a special Seer Stone that he would gaze into to be shown the future. This was a small, smooth rock that was small enough to be held in the hand. In the middle of the stone was a hole. Kenneth would look into this hole to be shown visions of the future. Whether his powers developed naturally and he used this seer stone as an aid, or whether this stone was magical and gave him his abilities is up for debate.

The stone itself has something of a strange origin story. Legend goes that Dark Kenneth's mother, before his birth, had seen spirits wandering around a nearby graveyard. His mother went out and stopped one of these spirits from going back to its grave. How she did this isn't known, but I like to imagine she just kept side stepping and stopping it from walking past like a very annoying person.

When she did finally agree to let this ghost go back to its grave — figuring it had probably been through enough what with having died already— the spirit gave her a gift. It was a small black and blue stone with a hole in the middle. This stone was given to Dark Kenneth when he was born. If this stone wasn't given to his irritating mother from the spirit realm, he may have just found it somewhere.

Powers Used For Bad News

Dark Kenneth didn't stay on Lewis for very long.

When he was old enough to work he moved to the Scottish Highlands and worked on the estates around Brahan Castle. It was during his time around Brahan Castle as an adolescent — and I like to think living up to his Dark Kenneth name by going through an edgy goth phase and listening to the eras equivalent of My Chemical Romance and dressing like the Crow — that his powers of prediction and second sight (seeing the future) started to gain popularity.

He would tell those around him of dreams and visions he had while gazing at his stone, and soon after they would come to pass.

It wasn't long before word of this psychic, this Brahan Seer, reached the ears of the Countess of Seaforth. The Countess lived in Brahan castle with her husband, the 3rd Earl of Seaforth.

The Countess was concerned for the wellbeing of her husband who was currently attending to whatever business Earls attended to in France in the 17th century. She sent for this Brahan Seer and asked him to use his abilities to tell her if her husband was okay.

The Brahan Seer agreed, and projected his mind across land and sea, all the way to Paris, where he found the Earl. "Is my husband well? Is he okay!?" the Countess asked. Dark Kenneth returned to his physical body from the astral realm, breathed deep to shake off the psychic exhaustion he had endured in completing this task, and finally answered; "Yeah. He's fine."

The Countess was glad to hear this comforting, if vague, answer. She asked The Brahan Seer for more information: where exactly was he? Who was he with? What was he doing? Poor Dark Kenneth should have kept his mouth shut.

He told The Countess that he had seen her husband in a bedroom in Paris with another woman. For some reason he decided to add that this woman was more attractive than her. Unsurprisingly, the Countess did not take this well. She was outraged. She didn't believe her husband would ever do such a thing. The Brahan Seer had no proof and no right to say these things about his better. She accused him of trying to defame The Earl.

She had The Brahan Seer arrested there and then, and taken to Chanory Point, a piece of land on the Moray Firth. There he was placed in a spiked barrel of tar and burned alive. A lesson for all psychics: if someone with the power to have you executed asks for your abilities, just give them the good news.

Before being executed, The Brahan Seer threw his seer stone, perhaps the source of his powers, into the waters of Loch Ussie. He claimed that someday a boy would be born with two navels. This boy would discover the stone inside the belly of a pike in the loch. This boy would then inherit the powers of second sight that once belonged to Dark Kenneth; essentially becoming *The Brahan Seer 2: Dark Kenneth Returns*.

The Prophecies

After The Brahan Seer's untimely death, many of the prophecies he told in life seemed to come true. Some shortly after, some taking decades, some centuries and some still coming to pass today.

One of the more well known prophecies involved a king being born but never crowned, and troublesome times at hand. Fairly vague, but the concept of an uncrowned king certainly captured the public's imaginations. Some say this prophecy did indeed come to pass in 1936 when Edward VIII abdicated before being crowned during the lead up to World War II. Troublesome times being at hand was an understatement.

Another prediction said that his home island of Lewis would be laid to waste. A similar prediction said that the entire island would sink. Either way, it might not be a good time to take a weekend break to Lewis.

As unlikely as these Lewis-based apocalyptic predictions seem, in 1997 a Scottish ecologist discovered that Lewis and several other islands nearby were sinking twice as fast as the mainland. If estimates are correct, then Lewis will be underwater in a couple of hundred thousand years. It's not the fastest resolving prediction, but The Brahan Seer does seem to be absolutely correct. Whether his prediction that the only survivors of this will be three nuns and a woman wearing red shoes remains to be seen.

A third prophecy mentions an island in the Outer Hebrides, North Uist, becoming populated by green men and grey geese. The green men, much to my disappointment, likely refer to soldiers and not aliens. Many islands in the Outer Hebrides have a military presence and even bases, it's not hard to imagine that North Uist will have one too someday, if not already.

The grey geese are much more straightforward. Literal geese have taken to wintering in many islands in the Outer Hebrides. Sometimes Dark

Kenneth is metaphorical, sometimes he's very literal.

Perhaps his most famous and, by far, most heavy metal prophecy refers to a black rain eating all things. But what does this black rain refer to? Could it be oil, a substance that has spawned a huge industry in Scotland? Could it be acid rain, the result of pollution that erodes much of what it touches? Could it even refer to the nuclear fallout from Chernobyl? Whatever it refers to, if it hasn't already come to pass, a black rain eating everything does not inspire much confidence in the future.

Was He Even Real?

In a twist of The Brahan Seer story worthy of any wizard, there is doubt that Dark Kenneth was ever a real person. There is absolutely no historical evidence or record of such a person ever existing.

A psychic making famous predictions and then, as a result, being executed seems like it would be a huge talking point, more than worthy enough for someone to write down. However, there is no mention of a Brahan Seer in any of the diaries found from this time period.

So if The Brahan Seer (AKA Dark Kenneth) wasn't a real person, then where does the story come from? Some believe that The Brahan Seer was created by Alexander Mackenzie for the 1877 book *The Prophecies Of The Brahan Seer*.

It is thought that Mackenzie created The Brahan Seer from two separate stories of two separate characters involved in second sight and witchcraft, who had appeared a century earlier. Sceptics think that Alexander combined these two people, took elements from both of their fantastical stories and created The Brahan Seer. Then, to give the story a Hollywood twist, decided to make The Countess the antagonist who has him killed.

His Legend Lives On

Despite the lack of historical evidence, fans of The Brahan Seer still firmly believe that he was a real person and possessed the ability to predict the future. Perhaps, they say, that after having Dark Kenneth executed The Countess ordered all records of his life erased.

The details of his life and the wealth of his predictions seem far too abundant to have simply been thought up by an author and lifted from other legends. The fact that his prophecies still have relevance today also speaks to Dark Kenneth's existence.

Perhaps the only way to know if the story of The Brahan Seer is true is if someone reading this book, a male, who was born with two navels, goes fishing in Loch Ussie. If they happen to catch a pike, look in its belly, find a stone with a hole in it, and suddenly gain the ability to see the future, then we will know for sure that not only was The Brahan Seer real, but he also had the powers he claimed.

Mary King's Close

We all know that a ghost is the spirit of a person that has passed away, but how is a ghost created? Many believe that ghosts stick around on the earthly plane due to some unfinished business that prevents them from entering the afterlife. Others believe that a horrific death can also keep a ghost tethered to our Earthly realm. This can explain why many sites where tragedy has befallen people have a reputation of being haunted.

Mary King's Close in Edinburgh could be considered one of these areas. It is a dark, cramped alleyway buried beneath the streets of Edinburgh right on the Royal Mile. The Close was sealed off for hundreds of years before being reopened in 2003 for people to visit and tour.

But why was it closed off? And do any of its old residents still remain?

A Brief History Lesson

In the 16th and 17th centuries Mary King's Close was one of the poorest areas to live in Edinburgh. As the city became more and more populated, it was unable to expand outwards to house its new residents due to the wall which surrounded it. Unable to get wider, the city got taller.

Buildings were quickly constructed in excess of eight stories high to house its ever growing population. The rich and upper class would occupy the higher levels, while the poor would be lower down, and even on street level. The rich had daylight and fresh air on the top, and the poor lived in the dark, dank, filthy streets at and near the bottom. These tall buildings formed two types of paths between them; wynds and closes.

Wynds were much like the streets of today. Public, open 24/7, and usable to anybody and everybody. Closes were a different story. Closes had gates on either end that were locked at night, keeping the residents in and everyone else out.

Mary King's Close was tight, claustrophobic and overcrowded. The unfortunate people who lived near the street level had to contend with some of the most unhygienic practices the time period had to offer. This was before the time of sewage systems so dirt, grime, and worse would simply flow through the streets like a river towards a large lake known as the Nor' Loch which was badly polluted with every gross thing you can imagine.

As if that wasn't bad enough, there were no toilets at this time. Edinburgh residents would simply do their business in a bucket and, when it was full, throw the contents out their windows and into the streets. This joined the ever growing river of stinking sludge that flowed through the city and right through Mary King's Close.

As you can imagine; this along with the cramped living conditions made disease prevalent in the Close. Flies and insects swarmed and rats roamed freely, loving these conditions.

In 1644 when The Black Death arrived in Edinburgh it quickly found a home. The Close was the perfect location for the plague to take hold and spread. And it spread fast.

When Edinburgh tried to combat the rapid spread of the plague, they quarantined the areas where it was most prevalent. Mary King's Close was closed off with most of its residents trapped inside, whether they had the plague or not. The gates, usually only locked at night, were locked permanently. Those left inside the Close had to survive on water and food passed in by kind passersby.

By 1645 Mary King's Close was abandoned. Some of the richer residents were able to leave on their own freewill as the plague loosened its stranglehold on the city, others simply died in the street, their corpses oozing puss, food for the very rats who gave them the fatal plague.

Close Quarters With The Dead

The Close lay empty for some years before people started to re-inhabit it, with the plague safely out of the city after killing between one fifth and one half of the population of Edinburgh.

In 1680 Thomas Coltheart, a lawyer, moved into a house in the Close with his family. The Coltheart family maid was moving some furniture into her employer's new home when a resident of the Close gave her a sinister and dire warning. She was told that if she and the family intended to stay there then "you will have more company than yourselves."

The ominous warning terrified the maid and she quickly told Mrs. Coltheart that her new home was haunted and that she would not be staying. The maid left, never to return. Mrs. Coltheart told her husband, worried about this supernatural information she had received, but he assured her there was no such thing as ghosts and that they would be staying in their new home that very night.

They did just that and nothing out of the ordinary happened. Mrs. Coltheart thought the maid had just overreacted to some gibberish from a local character. The next morning they went to church, but when they returned Mr. Coltheart began to feel unwell. He retired to bed to rest and his wife decided to sit in the living room and read the bible, having not gotten her fill of religion at church.

The wife sat across from the fire and opened the good book to her favourite psalm and dug in. After some time reading she glanced up at the fire and, from a small cupboard door above it, saw the disembodied head of a grey bearded old man appear. The shock was too much for Mrs. Coltheart and she fainted.

She came to some time later after hearing the neighbours entering their home loudly. The old man's ghostly head was no longer above the fireplace. She quickly rushed to her husband's bedside, shook him awake and told him what she had seen. Mr. Coltheart was sceptical. He told his wife it was simply a "delusion of her senses". What a great husband!

Later that night, after Mrs. Coltheart had gone to bed; still recovering from her ghostly shock earlier, Mr. Coltheart decided to sit up by the fire, unable to sleep after his earlier nap. He was shocked when the same disembodied head appeared, seemingly staring right at him. He rushed to the bedroom, woke his wife, told her what he'd seen, and received a big fat "told you so!" before they both began to pray.

It wasn't long before the old man's head joined them in the bedroom. They continued to pray. Soon after the apparition of a young boy wearing a coat joined the floating head. They lit candles, and still prayed. Next, an arm appeared. It was positioned as if giving a salute. It floated towards the couple who climbed into bed to retreat. They prayed some more.

Next appeared a phantom dog. It looked around the room, at the bed, at Mr. and Mrs. Coltheart, at the other ghosts in the room, then jumped up onto a chair for a snooze. Still, they prayed. Next a ghostly cat appeared and jumped around the room. More praying followed. In the hallway they could see small creatures dancing; creatures that they couldn't even begin to describe. They danced their way into the bedroom. The Colthearts, having tried everything else, decided praying was a good idea. Suddenly, while praying harder than they had ever prayed before, their ears were assaulted by a loud and dreadful groan that they described as sounding like "a strong man dying". As the groan ended, all their ghostly visitors vanished.

The couple were relieved when the spirits left, and even more relieved when they never returned. Despite this terrifying encounter, and as the ghosts were seemingly gone forever, Mr. and Mrs Coltheart decided to stay in their new home.

Some years later, a client of Thomas Coltheart who lived ten miles outside of Edinburgh was awoken by a human shaped cloud-like entity walking around his bedroom. He jumped out of bed and grabbed his sword. As he prepared to cut down this strange cloud being, its face became more defined and recognisable. It was the face of Thomas Coltheart. The man asked the cloud with the face of Coltheart if he was dead. It shook its head twice, and melted away into nothing.

The client started at once for Edinburgh, to see his lawyer and find an answer to the apparition in his bedroom. When he arrived at the Coltheart home, he found Mrs. Coltheart mourning her husband's death. Thomas Coltheart, it was discovered, had died at almost the exact time the client had the strange encounter.

It seemed that in death Mr. Coltheart had joined the ranks of the spectres that had once troubled him. If you can't beat 'em.

Let The Living In

In the 1750's Edinburgh Council decided to build the new Royal Exchange building on the location of Mary King's Close. The few residents who remained in the Close at this time were finally convinced to leave so construction could start.

Rather than demolish everything though, the city simply destroyed the top floors and used the lower levels as a foundation for the new Exchange building. The homes left on these lower levels were left buried and untouched for 250 years.

In 2003 what remained of Mary King's Close was opened to the public, after historians and archeologists had had their fill. Quickly tales of paranormal encounters started to flood out. A woman in black is one of the frequently reported ghosts seen in the Close, with many believing it's the spirit of Mary King herself. In life Mary was a fabric merchant and successful business woman who lived and worked in the Close. Does her spirit now wander the subterranean street which now bears her name?

Inside an old chimney where, according to legend, a young chimney sweep perished, whispers and scratching sounds can be heard inside. A few people brave enough to have stuck their faces into this chimney have come away with scratches caused by something unseen in the darkness.

A ghost of a grumpy old man is frequently seen skulking around at street level. People believe this to be Andrew Chesney, the last resident of Mary King's Close, before he was forced to move out in 1902. Andrew was known to be particularly proud of his toilet and would often use it with the door open, waving to passersby.

Phantom sounds are heard, with no known cause. Shadows are seen moving in the dim light. Cold spots are felt throughout without reason. Visitors are grabbed and pushed.

Perhaps the most famous modern paranormal tale from Mary King's Close is that of Annie.

In 1992, before the Close was officially opened, a psychic was able to get special access to the buried area beneath the Exchange. The area was alive with energy, but as she walked from ancient house to house, there was one room that the psychic simply could not bring herself to enter. She experienced an intense feeling of dread and then the very physical feeling of someone pulling on her trousers.

Soon after, the psychic was able to return to this room and discover what had caused this feeling. In the room she found the ghost of a 9 year old girl. The girl was sad as she couldn't find her family. Many have theorised that the young girl was abandoned by her family, due to her catching the plague. The girl also told the psychic she was sad because she couldn't find her doll. The psychic named the girl Annie, bought her a doll from the surface world, returned to the room and left it there for her.

When Mary King's Close opened to the public, many followed this psychics' example, bringing Annie dolls and leaving them in her room. The room now contains a small mountain of dolls and cuddly toys as a memorial to Annie.

A Ghosts Perfect Home

Is Mary King's Close haunted by the ghosts of former residents and victims of The Black Death? Can the strange encounters just be explained away as people overreacting to being in a spooky location? Or could something truly supernatural be at work here?

If you believe that ghosts are the spirits of people who died in horrible, violent, or unjust ways, then Mary King's Close could be considered a perfect location for the creation of some ghosts. The whole area seems to check every box on the list when it comes to "best areas to haunt". The people who lived there had hard lives, endured terrible conditions, then died in one of the worst ways imaginable. If anyone was going to stick around after dying, it was going to be these people.

If there was a location where ghosts were bound to exist, can you think of a better place than Mary King's Close?

The Gurning Man

Gurning has a strange place in Scotland. This act of contorting one's face into a grotesque and menacing grimace has inspired competitions, contests, and even a world championship where contestants pull and stretch their faces into the most inhuman visage. These competitions have found a niche following not just in Scotland, not just in the UK, but the world over.

Ask anyone in Scotland about gurning and they'll likely tell you how their grandad would pull funny faces to make them laugh when they were young. For an area of Glasgow in the 1970s though, gurning would take on a far more sinister and terrifying meaning.

A Strange Man Appears

In the Crosshill area of Glasgow in 1976, two teenage girls were walking home late one night after a party. It was dark, and their way was illuminated by streetlights. Under a streetlight ahead of them, they saw the figure of a man. They described the man as being tall, thin, in his 50s, bald and wearing tight black clothing that appeared to be one piece, like a cat suit.

The girls thought this was strange but continued onwards, keen to get home. As they got closer to the man they realised he was jittering and shaking, but standing in place. He almost looked like a glitching video game character. The girls stopped their conversation and quickened their pace, desperate to get past this jittery man as soon as possible. As the girls passed him they tried not to make eye contact, but they were able to see his face in their peripheral vision. It was contorted in a gurn that the girls described as somewhere between an amused grin and look of sheer pain. As they passed they could hear him breathing heavily and grunting.

As soon as they were clear of him, the girls started running. After putting a small distance between themselves and this gurning man, they looked back. He was gone. There was nowhere he could have run to in such a short period of time, and there was nowhere for him to be hiding. It was as if he had simply vanished. The girls had no idea what to do and contacted the police. They found no trace of the strange gurning man.

This wasn't the last time The Gurning Man would be seen, or the last time the police would be contacted about him.

A few nights later, in a house near where the girls saw him, The Gurning Man appeared again. It was once again late at night, and a married couple were asleep in their bed. The wife was awoken by a strange grunting sound from the end of the bed. This surprised her, as the strange grunting in the bedroom usually came from her husband, but he was fast asleep beside her.

She slowly looked up, and was shocked by what she saw. Illuminated by the moonlight, at the end of the bed, she saw a tall, skinny, bald man in tight black clothes gurning at her while robotically rubbing his chest. Naturally, the woman screamed, waking her husband who bolted to the lightswitch. He turned the lights on, but the room was empty apart from him and his wife.

They called the police, thinking it was an intruder who had broken into their home. The police found no evidence of anyone breaking in, and could not explain how someone could have escaped so quickly.

Just a few days after this couple's encounter with The Gurning Man, he appeared again. An elderly woman was putting out some milk bottles in the early morning. As she was placing the bottles down outside her front door, something in the street caught her eye.

In the middle of the street she saw a tall, thin, bald man in black clothing running in place. As he ran without actually moving forward, he pulled a series of disturbing, contorted faces at her. The old woman was confused, and just as she thought about going inside to call the police, he disappeared before her very eyes.

From 1976 to 1979 The Gurning Man was seen a total of 17 reported times, though there may be more encounters that were never shared. The Gurning Man was always seen either late at night or early in the morning, when it was nice and dark and not many people were around. Of the reported sightings, 11 took place outdoors while 6 were inside people's homes. Of the encounters inside of houses, nothing was ever stolen and no sign of a break in could ever be found.

It seemed that after 1979 The Gurning Man simply vanished as quickly and as mysteriously as he had arrived. But was he gone for good?

The Gurning Returns

In 2017, two new possible sightings of The Gurning Man were reported in areas very close to Crosshill.

The first involved a young woman walking home at night after seeing some friends. As she made her way along a street close to Queens Park, she saw a figure standing between the parked vehicles at the roadside. She described him as old, spindly, and wearing tight black clothes. As she got closer to him, she heard he was making strange snorting and grunting sounds and saw that he was rubbing his chest in a jittery motion.

The second report came from a group of teenage girls who claimed to have seen The Gurning Man in Queens Park itself. They were sitting on a bench in the park at night when suddenly they heard some strange noises and saw movement in a nearby bush. One of the girls turned on the torch on her mobile phone and shone it at the shrubbery. As she did, The Gurning Man emerged. They described him as we've come to expect; old, tall, thin, bald, black clothing, and moving very oddly. The girls got the shock of their lives when this figure emerged from the bush — and they fled the park.

Theories & Connection To Point Pleasant

Who, or what was, (or is) The Gurning Man? Where did he, or it, come from? And what did this person or creature want?

Was The Gurning Man some sort of ghost, spirit, or even a demon? If so, why did it appear simply to torment the people of Crosshill? Was The Gurning Man an extra-dimensional entity — a humanoid creature from a different but similar world that would occasionally slip into our reality through some sort of dimensional wormhole before being sucked back through? Was The Gurning Man of alien origin? A creature from outer space sent to gather data on the human race? Was it simply wearing a human costume and attempting to blend in but not quite getting the hang of it?

The Gurning Man shares many similarities with an entity known as The Grinning Man who was seen in Point Pleasant, West Virginia, just ten years earlier and is connected to the events of the world famous strange occurrences that took place there.

From late 1966 until the end of 1967 Point Pleasant seemed to be sitting directly on a tear in the dimensional veil. Not only was a large, black, anthropomorphic moth with a giant wingspan and glowing red eyes — the Mothman — sighted by an enormous amount of people, the town was besieged by all sorts of strange entities. Residents saw UFOs, reported poltergeist activity, and watched as Men in Black stalked the town asking locals weird questions and were generally their unnerving selves. In addition to these unexplained occurrences, there was The Grinning Man.

The Grinning Man, also known as Indrid Cold, first appeared November 2, 1966. Woodrow Derenberger was driving home on a long and deserted road when he heard a crash. He stopped his car, thinking it may have somehow been damaged. There was no other vehicle on the road that the sound could have come from. As soon as he stepped on the brakes however, a strange craft descended from the sky and landed in front of his parked car. He described this UFO as looking like an old kerosene lamp. Things were about to get stranger for Woodrow.

A man, or something that looked like a man, exited the craft. He was described as being tall, tanned, having small beady eyes, slicked back hair, and a large creepy grin. He walked up to Woodrow's car and spoke to him telepathically, without moving his lips. He told Woodrow that his name was Indrid Cold, that he was from another planet, he called himself a "Searcher", and said would meet with Woodrow again. He did indeed meet with him again.

Woodrow met Indrid mere weeks before the arrival of Mothman, and not too far from the town of Point Pleasant. The events are widely speculated to be linked somehow.

Both The Gurning Man and The Grinning Man are described as tall, thin, and wearing tight dark clothing. Both are also known for their expressions; creepy and exaggerated grins. While descriptions of their appearance do vary slightly, and it may be far-fetched to claim that they are the same entity, they could be related. Perhaps they came from the same place, wherever that may be.

The Grinning Man also seemed to have a different motivation than his gurning cousin. Indrid would deliver messages, admittedly cryptic ones, to Woodrow. The Gurning Man seemed incapable of this and appeared to be more interested in simply scaring those who saw him. Additionally, The Grinning Man appeared to have a connection to the Men in Black, though whether he was working with or against them is hotly debated.

Perhaps strange men in black suits were seen in Glasgow in the late 70s too, investigating the Gurning Man but simply went unnoticed and unreported due to the terror that this tall, thin, bald man was causing.

Nessie's Exorcism

I know what you're thinking. You read the title 'Nessie's Exorcism' and now you're thinking "We're near the end of the book now, he's out of stories and he's just making stuff up."

First of all, I'm insulted. Second of all, despite this sounding like the title of a SyFy channel movie — they still haven't got back to me about my *Mothmanipede Versus Chupacabtron* idea — this is a real story. While some of the accounts and characters may be questionable, an exorcism was indeed attempted at Loch Ness with the purpose of banishing the evil spirit of The Loch Ness Monster.

Nessie Super Fan

Ted Holiday, a journalist and cryptozoologist who wrote about ghosts, aliens, cryptids and... fishing, was obsessed with Nessie. In 1962, he joined the Loch Ness Phenomena Investigation Bureau and spent hundreds of hours over the next few years watching the loch and hoping to catch a glimpse of the monster. He claims that in his countless hours staring at the loch he saw Nessie a grand total of four times. Or he, at least, had four sightings of something he was unable to explain.

In 1968, Holiday released a book titled *The Great Orm Of Loch Ness*, in which he explained his theory that Nessie was some form of giant prehistoric invertebrate. Basically Holiday was under the impression that Nessie was an ancient and gigantic version of today's common garden slug. He believed this type of creature was once plentiful in the UK and was the basis for the legend of dragons. He theorised that these creatures had all but died out, save the one living in Loch Ness.

While Holiday believed that Nessie was a flesh and blood creature, he also theorised about its paranormal abilities. He began to reject the idea that monsters were simply undiscovered animals that had eluded science. He started to believe that perhaps they were something far stranger. In 1968, the year his book was released, he spoke about how Nessie appeared to several locals in a clear area of the loch. They tried to snap pictures of the monster, but each of them experienced problems with their cameras. None of the pictures came out, and photographic proof of Nessie was once again lost.

In his later books and writings, Holiday theorised that all aspects of the paranormal were connected. His theory was that although Nessie was a real creature, it had paranormal abilities — abilities that helped hide its existence. This theory could explain why most photos of allegedly real paranormal events and creatures usually turn out blurry or distorted.

Shortly after the release of his book, Holiday read another book that had a different opinion of Nessie. Former reverend Doctor Donald Omand was of the opinion that Nessie was more of a spiritual creature; something like a ghost or spectre. Holiday began writing to Omand and the two quickly bonded over their shared interest in Loch Ness, its monster, and other elements of the paranormal.

Omand invited Holiday to come visit him at his house in Devon. It was during this visit that Doctor Omand shared his opinion that Loch Ness needed to be exorcised of the evil spirit that haunted its waters, and that he was the man to do it. Omand, as it turned out, was quite an accomplished exorcist. He had travelled all over the world performing exorcisms and specialised, uniquely, in casting evil spirits out of circus tents and wild animals possessed by demons. It's good to have a niche.

Holiday agreed to join Omand when he performed his exorcism of Loch Ness. The two of them met on the shores of the loch on June 2nd, 1973.

A Watery Exorcism

Four locations along the banks of Loch Ness were selected for where the exorcism would be performed. Holiday, Omand, along with a driver, and two other individuals, travelled around the loch and at each of the four points the Reverend Doctor performed the same ritual. During the exorcism speech, Omand referred to Nessie as a serpent and called on God to rid the loch of all evil spirits. All seemed to be going well, until they had to perform the last stage of the exorcism in the centre of the loch.

In a small boat, the exorcism party sailed out into the middle of Loch Ness. Omand began the exorcism finale over 7000 feet of cold, dark water. During this last stage, Omand called for the serpent to reveal itself and be cloaked no more. Holiday described feeling an increasing tension in the air. He said he was sure that Nessie, either as an evil spirit or in the flesh (or scales) was going to make an appearance, and he was particularly worried that it might try to attack the small boat.

Holiday, Omand, and the rest of The Exorcism Crew, held their collective breaths. Mist drifted across the still surface of the loch. An owl hooted. The boat rocked. And then, without warning... nothing happened.

Nessie chose to remain cloaked despite the Doctor's best efforts. Omand did collapse at the end of the ritual, something he had told Holiday happens at the end of every successful exorcism. Thus the Loch Ness exorcism was deemed a success and they paddled the boat back to shore. It's a shame they didn't have time to visit Boleskine, maybe they could have cleaned up some of Crowley's demonic mess.

Only The Beginning

Omand spent the next day resting, exhausted from his collapse. Then on June 5th, they staged a re-enactment for the media during the day. On the night of the 5th, something very strange happened to Holiday.

Holiday was relaxing in the sitting room of Mrs. Cary, whose home he and Omand were staying at during their Loch Ness adventure. They had a caravan on their property, but spent much of the time in the house speaking to Mrs. and Mr. Cary. On this day he was telling Mrs. Cary and her husband that he planned to visit a nearby location where a landed UFO had been seen. Three tall occupants wearing what looked like diving suits entered the craft before it took off. The witness to this strange craft, a Swedish journalist, claimed that afterwards he was harassed by the Men in Black until he suffered a full nervous breakdown.

Mrs. Cary warned Holiday not to go, worried that something might happen to him if he did. It was a warning he also received from Omand when he told him of his plan. As soon as Mrs. Cary had finished her warning, Holiday heard what he described as a rushing sound outside. He looked out the window, which was behind Mrs. Cary, and saw a dark mass of smoke appear. It was shaped like a pyramid and was around 8 feet high, swirling quickly like a tornado. Bangs and crashes shook the house to such an extent that Holiday feared that the building was collapsing.

Holiday looked out the window again and saw a rosebush in the garden trying to tear itself out of the ground. The whole strange experience lasted only 15 seconds, and although Holiday and Mrs. Cary both saw and heard things, her husband did not.

Later, Holiday asked Mrs. Cary to recount what she had experienced, curious to see if it matched up to his own. Mrs. Cary described how herself and Holiday were discussing a nearby UFO sighting when she heard some loud crashes around the house. She had the impression that someone or something was at the window behind her, but she couldn't look around. She then saw a beam of white light shine through the window and land on Holiday's forehead, exactly where Omand had made a cross of holy water two days before, prior to the exorcism, for protection.

The Man in Black

The morning after this unusual incident, Holiday left the Cary house to go get some things from the caravan. As he turned the corner of the house towards the caravan, which was at the top of a slope leading down to Loch Ness, he stopped in his tracks. Beside the caravan, facing Holiday, with his back to the loch, was a strange man. A man dressed entirely in black.

Holiday knew that this man was no tourist here to admire the beauty of Loch Ness. He was hardly dressed for it, and he wasn't even interested in looking at the loch behind him. It seemed as if he was simply standing there, waiting for Holiday. As is the case in many Men in Black encounters, Holiday felt an intense feeling of malevolence coming from the figure.

After staring at the MIB for a few seconds, Holiday decided to slowly approach him. He described him as being 6 feet tall, and dressed in a black leather or plastic; like Klaus Nomi. He also wore a black helmet, black gloves, and goggles. The goggles had lenses that would have covered the man's eyes, though Holiday could see no eyes behind the lenses.

Holiday walked slowly past him, and he remained motionless. Holiday then took a few steps beyond him and looked down at Loch Ness. He stayed as silent as he could, but could hear no noise from the man. Not even breathing. Holiday started to doubt that this Man in Black was even real, and formed a plan where he'd pretend to slip and fall when he walked back past him, hoping to make some sort of contact and see if he had a physical presence.

As Holiday built up the courage to turn around and pretend to fall on this man, he heard a bizarre whispering sound and quickly turned around. The goggled man was gone. A huge area was visible to Holiday, but the MIB was nowhere to be seen. There was no way any human could have run out of sight that quickly (or silently). One year later, while visiting the same spot, Holliday suffered a heart attack.

A Universe of Goblins

In the space of just a few days, Ted Holiday had experienced quite the paranormal adventure: meeting with a Man in Black after witnessing an exorcism of a cryptid which resulted in poltergeist activity while discussing a UFO. If there was a bingo card, I think that would be a full house.

It's no wonder that Holiday later tried to find a connection between all aspects of the paranormal in his book *The Goblin Universe*. In this book he theorised that cryptids, UFOs, ghosts, Men in Black, and everything else you can imagine all come from the same place. He tried to find connections between encounters with all different types of phenomenon and the weird synchronicities that seem to come with all of them.

Although the book was debatably disowned by Holiday and was only published posthumously, there's no denying that it certainly contains some interesting ideas and is a valiant effort to try and explain and find a connection between all aspects of the paranormal. No easy job!

Holiday's theory of all paranormal phenomena being related may not be too far from the truth. Can it be pure coincidence he encountered the gambit of the paranormal in just a few days?

Could Nessie be the spirit of a cryptid that attacked Holiday after the attempted exorcism, only to be repelled by the protective cross of holy water that was made on his head? And why did it attack when he was discussing a UFO sighting? Is Nessie, or Nessies spirit, somehow connected to extraterrestrials? Did the Man in Black appear due to Holiday's interest in the UFO sighting? Or because of his involvement in the Nessie exorcism? Or both? And what did the MIB want? Was it there to intimidate Holiday? Or was it and its ridiculous appearance a way to discredit Holidays research and throw him off the case? Holiday did keep his MIB encounter to himself for some time afterwards, well aware of how strange the incident sounded and how weird his description of the "man" would be.

Once again we're left with the questions who are the MIB, where are they from, and who are they working for? They seem too strange to be simple government agents, sent out to keep witnesses of the paranormal quiet — and their own seemingly paranormal abilities put them outside the realm of what we know mere G-men to be capable of.

Was this Man in Black, in his weird helmet, one of the same figures in diving suits that were said to have entered the UFO seen near the loch? Could Loch Ness be another area where the veil between this world and another world, or Goblin Universe, is thin? Could entities of all shapes and sizes, from prehistoric dinosaur looking ghosts to crafts that look like they came from outer space, to tall humanoid people dressed entirely in black, easily slip through and sometimes interact with people of this reality before slipping back without a trace?

Epilogue

So there we have it; some stories that just scrape the surface of Scotland's weird history, from the distant past right up to the present day. I hope that after reading this collection you now agree that Scotland can easily be ranked amongst the strangest places on Earth.

But rest assured, this isn't just a gathering of unexplained stories that have happened in Scotland, many of these stories are still happening. UFOs are still being spotted in the Falkirk Triangle, Morag is still sighted traversing her loch, Boleskine is ready to spring back into occult action at any minute, The Gurning Man appears to be making a return, and a breakthrough could come through in The Livingston Encounter and Nessie's Exorcism cases anytime. You never know when a small but vital piece of evidence will be found.

A new phantom could appear on the Ghost Road, The Trouble might pick a new family to torment, and The Grey Man may chase another hiker all the way back down Ben McDhui. Any and all of the stories you've read in this book could find new life at any moment. And, with all we now know about tulpas, a new element is added to these tales. If enough people read about them, believe them, and inadvertently project their psychic energy into them, then who knows what can become reality?

And that isn't to mention all the great stories that are currently happening or about to happen that we haven't heard of yet. With so much unexplainable supernatural mystery in Scotland, it's hard to believe that someone isn't seeing a UFO, battling with a poltergeist, experimenting with the dark arts, or dealing with the Men in Black right now.

It's only a matter of time until these stories come to light and Scotland becomes even more Unexplained.

Acknowledgements

This book would not exist without those who have tirelessly researched these subjects before me. The people who do what I only pretend to. The people who are there, on the scene, interviewing people. The people who read hundreds of pages of dull documentation and try to make sense of it. The people who go through the historic evidence and put it all in context. The real Mulders and the unsung heroes of the paranormal.

A full list of the main sources by chapter can be found at the end of this book, but I would like to give special mention to Colin Wilson, Nick Redfern, John Keel, Jack Strange, The Paranormal Database, Spooky Isles, Folklore Scotland, Undiscovered Scotland and Last Podcast On The Left.

I'd also like to give a special special mention to Ron Halliday whose books were a constant source of amazing information and inspiration. Entire chapters of this book, like The East Kilbride Goblin and The Blairgowrie UFOs, simply would not exist without his research and writing on these subjects. *Paranormal Scotland, McX, UFO Scotland* and *Haunted Glasgow* were all fantastic resources while writing this book.

Thanks to Fraser for the author photo (and making me look much cooler than I really do).

Thanks to Laura and Ella for helping with the book every step of the way and not having me sectioned when I thought the Men in Black were trying to interfere with its writing (they were).

Thanks to Matt for the incredible cover art.

Thanks to mum and dad for encouraging me to be the weirdo we all know today.

Thanks to my friends for the crazy amount of support I received when I said I was writing this bizarre book.

And finally, thank you.

Thanks for taking a chance on a book that admittedly has a limited and niche appeal. I truly hope you enjoyed it.

About The Author

Photography by Fraser Kerr

"The Men in Black have tapped my phone again."

Martin R. Shaw is a writer and paranormal enthusiast from the North East of Scotland.

He developed a fascination (some say obsession) with the supernatural at a young age after being exposed to cheesy paranormal recreation shows and X-Files marathons.

He writes about UFOs, cryptids and ghosts in a fun and engaging style, including plenty of jokes and pop culture references along the way.

Bibliography

Aleister Crowley & Boleskine House

1. https://en.wikipedia.org/wiki/Boleskine_House
2. https://www.scotsman.com/regions/inverness-highlands-and-islands/jimmy-page-and-his-black-magic-highland-home-1487080
3. https://faroutmagazine.co.uk/boleskine-house-aleister-crowley-jimmy-page-portal-to-hell/
4. https://www.compulsiononline.com/people_crowley3.htm
5. The A-Z of Paranormal Scotland - Ron Halliday: Page 27
6. McX - Ron Halliday: Page 177
7. The Real Men in Black - Nick Redfern: Page 78
8. Raising Hell - Robert Masello: Page 119
9. Lucifer Rising - Gavin Baddeley: Page 96
10. Season of the Witch - Peter Bebergal: Page 93
11. The Dark History of the Occult - Paul Roland: Page 98
12. Aleister Crowley - Gary Lachman: Page 72

Bonnybridge & Zalus

1.https://www.heraldscotland.com/business_hq/23933383.stranger-things-usual-happening-forth-valley/
2. The A-Z of Paranormal Scotland - Ron Halliday: Page 30, 316
3. McX - Ron Halliday: Page 10
4. UFO Scotland - Ron Halliday: Page 186
5. UFO Case Files of Scotland - Malcolm Robinson: Page 97

6. The UFO Investigators Handbook - Marc Gascoigne: Page 123
7. Paranormal Encounters on Britain's Roads - Peter A. McCue: Page 107

The Grey Man

1. https://en.wikipedia.org/wiki/Am_Fear_Liath_M%C3%B2r
2. https://www.undiscoveredscotland.co.uk/usscotfax/outdoors/greyman.html
3. https://weewhitehoose.co.uk/study/am-fear-liath-mor-scotlands-yeti/
4. https://www.icysedgwick.com/grey-man-of-ben-macdui/
5. The A-Z of Paranormal Scotland - Ron Halliday: Page 127
6. McX - Ron Halliday: Page 102
7. Strange Tales of Scotland - Jack Strange: Page 93

The Glasgow Witches

1. https://folklorescotland.com/the-witches-of-pollok-house/
2. https://hiddenscotland.com/journal/pollock-witch-hunts
3. https://www.glasgowlive.co.uk/news/history/pollok-witches-hysteria-trials-1677-17156251
4. Haunted Glasgow - Ron Halliday: Page 126

The Wizard of Yester

1. https://en.wikipedia.org/wiki/Yester_Castle
2. https://en.wikipedia.org/wiki/Hugh_de_Giffard
3. https://whiteadder.aocarchaeology.com/stories-and-ballads/myths-and-legends/goblin-sighting-at-yester-house/
4. https://winsham.blogspot.com/2015/09/wednesday-weirdness-magic-of-yester.html
5. https://www.edinburghlive.co.uk/best-in-edinburgh/whats-on-news/hidden-below-ruins-yester-castle-17666071
6. Strange Tales of Scotland - Jack Strange: Page 124

A75: The Ghost Road

1. https://en.wikipedia.org/wiki/A75_road
2. https://www.bbc.co.uk/news/uk-scotland-south-scotland-24655488
3. https://www.mysteriousbritain.co.uk/hauntings/a75-kinmount-straight/
4. https://www.spookyisles.com/scotlands-a75-the-haunted-road/
5. Paranormal Encounters on Britain's Roads - Peter A. McCue: Page 50

The Blairgowrie UFOs

1. The A-Z of Paranormal Scotland - Ron Halliday: Page 21

2. McX - Ron Halliday: Page 35
3. UFO Scotland - Ron Halliday: Page 125
4. https://www.dumbartonreporter.co.uk/news/18624883.ufo-special-seven-strang-est-unexplained-sightings-scotlands-skies/

The Trouble at Ringcroft

1. https://en.wikipedia.org/wiki/Auchencairn
2. https://www.scotsman.com/heritage-and-retro/heritage/the-story-of-the-galloway-poltergeist-that-terrified-a-community-and-burned-down-a-farmhouse-1403661
3. https://www.goblinshead.co.uk/bogles/ring-croft-of-stocking/
4. https://www.mysteriousbritain.co.uk/hauntings/rerrick-poltergeist-1695/
5. https://en.wikipedia.org/wiki/Bell_Witch
6. https://sharetngov.tnsosfiles.com/tsla/exhibits/myth/bellwitch.htm
7. The A-Z of Paranormal Scotland - Ron Halliday: Page 252
8. McX - Ron Halliday: Page 167
9. An Illustrated History of Ghosts - Adam Allsuch Boardman: Page 44

The Flannan Lighthouse Mystery

1. https://en.wikipedia.org/wiki/Flannan_Isles_Lighthouse
2. https://allthatsinteresting.com/flannan-isle-mystery
3. https://www.historic-uk.com/HistoryUK/HistoryofScotland/The-Eilean-Mor-Light-house-Mystery/
4. https://www.strangeoutdoors.com/historical-strangeness/category/Eilean+mor+light-house
5. The A-Z of Paranormal Scotland - Ron Halliday: Page 252
6. McX - Ron Halliday: Page 98
7. World Famous Strange Tales & Weird Mysteries - Colin & Damon Wilson: Page 32

Netta & Iona

1. https://www.mysteriousbritain.co.uk/occult/netta-fornario-ionas-occult-mystery/
2. https://medium.com/@anncarney51/the-strange-death-of-netta-fornario-b4d6817d-7e6f
3. https://www.strangeoutdoors.com/historical-strangeness/netta-fornario
4. The A-Z of Paranormal Scotland - Ron Halliday: Page 149, 237
5. McX - Ron Halliday: Page 232
6. Encyclopedia of Occult and Supernatural Murder - Brian Lane: Page 113

The Livingston Encounter

1. https://en.wikipedia.org/wiki/Robert_Taylor_incident

2. https://www.bbc.co.uk/news/uk-scotland-50262655
3. https://www.undiscoveredscotland.co.uk/livingston/livingstonincident/index.html
4. The A-Z of Paranormal Scotland - Ron Halliday: Page 171
5. McX - Ron Halliday: Page 3
6. UFO Scotland - Ron Halliday: Page 2
7. UFOs The Definitive Casebook - John Spencer: Page 110

The Egyptian Bone

1. https://www.mysteriousbritain.co.uk/hauntings/cursed-bone-of-learmonth-gardens/
2. https://www.british-paranormal.co.uk/lady-setons-cairo-curse-edinburgh/
3. https://seeksghosts.blogspot.com/2012/12/haunted-object-cursed-egyptian-bone.html
4. Strange Tales of Scotland - Jack Strange: Page 54

The East Kilbride Goblin

1. https://www.history.com/news/little-green-men-origins-aliens-hopkinsville-kelly
2. https://cryptidz.fandom.com/wiki/Hopkinsville_Goblins
3. The A-Z of Paranormal Scotland - Ron Halliday: Page 117
4. The Inhumanoids - Marton M. Nunnelly: Page 255
5. UFOs The Definitive Casebook - John Spencer: Page 36
6. The A-Z of Paranormal Scotland - Ron Halliday: Page 117

The A70 Abduction

1. https://www.spookyisles.com/a70-ufo-incident-scotland/
2. https://www.edinburghlive.co.uk/news/edinburgh-news/ufo-a70-incident-saw-aliens-25919992
3. https://www.ufocasebook.com/a70abduction.html
4. https://www.scotsman.com/news/mod-took-alien-abduction-of-scots-duo-seriously-according-to-secret-file-1618160
5. The A-Z of Paranormal Scotland - Ron Halliday: Page 303
6. McX - Ron Halliday: Page 21
7. UFO Scotland - Ron Halliday: Page 214
8. Paranormal Encounters on Britain's Roads - Peter A. McCue: Page 118
9. The A70 UFO Incident - Malcolm Robinson

Mary King's Close

1. https://www.atlasobscura.com/places/mary-kings-close
2. https://eerieedinburgh.com/spooky-stories/f/ghosts-of-mary-kings-close-edinburghs-eerie-underworld
3. The A-Z of Paranormal Scotland - Ron Halliday: Page 177

Bibliography

4. McX - Ron Halliday: Page 91

The Bargarran Possession

1. https://en.wikipedia.org/wiki/Christian_Shaw
2. https://en.wikipedia.org/wiki/Paisley_witches
3. https://www.glasgowlive.co.uk/news/history/bargarran-witch-trials-1697-14162436
4. https://www.paisleysenchantedthreads.co.uk/the-story/the-events/
5. https://www.amusingplanet.com/2022/01/the-witches-of-paisley.html
6. The A-Z of Paranormal Scotland - Ron Halliday: Page 16
7. Haunted Glasgow - Ron Halliday: Page 132

Morag: The Monster of Loch Morar

1. https://www.scottish-at-heart.com/morag-loch-morar.html
2. https://www.scotclans.com/pages/morag-the-monster
3. https://cryptidz.fandom.com/wiki/Morag
4. The A-Z of Paranormal Scotland - Ron Halliday: Page 192
5. McX - Ron Halliday: Page 154
6. Strange Tales of Scotland - Jack Strange: Page 27

The Calvine UFO Photo

1. https://en.wikipedia.org/wiki/Calvine_UFO
2. https://drdavidclarke.co.uk/2022/08/12/the-calvine-ufo-revealed/
3. https://drdavidclarke.co.uk/secret-files/the-calvine-ufo-photographs/
4. UFO Drawings From The National Archives - David Clarke: Page 104
5. Fortean Times - FT423

Robert Gordon & The Devil

1. https://spookyscotland.net/wizard-of-gordonstoun/
2. https://www.spookyisles.com/the-wizard-of-gordonstoun/
3. https://gordoncastles.fandom.com/wiki/Gordonstoun

Edinburgh's Tiny Coffins

1. https://www.icysedgwick.com/edinburgh-miniature-coffins/
2. https://mymacabreroadtrip.com/edinburgh-miniature-coffins/
3. https://www.edinburghnews.scotsman.com/news/people/the-arthurs-seat-coffins-the-strange-edinburgh-mystery-linked-to-burke-and-hare-and-witchcraft-4097904

4. https://www.mentalfloss.com/article/524144/enigma-edinburghs-miniature-coffins
5. The A-Z of Paranormal Scotland - Ron Halliday: Page 51
6. McX - Ron Halliday: Page 226

The Gorbals Vampire

1. https://www.davidcastleton.net/gorbals-vampire-glasgow-southern-necropolis/
2. https://folklorescotland.com/the-gorbals-vampire/
3. https://www.heraldscotland.com/news/14695521.back-dead-ghastly-tale-gorbals-vampire/
4. https://www.glasgowworld.com/retro/gorbals-vampire-explained-was-the-glasgow-folklore-monster-real-3891719
5. https://www.mentalfloss.com/article/650659/scotland-gorbals-vampire-hunt
6. https://spookyscotland.net/gorbals-vampire/

The Brahan Seer

1. https://en.wikipedia.org/wiki/Brahan_Seer
2. https://www.historic-uk.com/HistoryUK/HistoryofScotland/The-Brahan-Seer-the-Scottish-Nostradamus/
3. https://www.scotclans.com/pages/brahan-seer
https://www.mysteriousbritain.co.uk/folklore/the-brahan-seer/
4. The A-Z of Paranormal Scotland - Ron Halliday: Page 38
5. McX - Ron Halliday: Page 117
6. Strange Tales of Scotland - Jack Strange: Page 86

The Gurning Man

1. https://www.spookyisles.com/gurning-man-glasgow/
2. https://www.glasgowlive.co.uk/news/glasgow-news/glasgow-ghosts-meet-gurning-man-20266535
3. https://www.british-paranormal.co.uk/the-gurning-man-of-glasgow/
4. https://dailyyonder.com/woodrow-derenberger-and-the-legend-of-indrid-cold/2021/12/03/
5. https://www.encyclopedia.com/science/encyclopedias-almanacs-transcripts-and-maps/derenberger-woodrow
6. https://cryptidz.fandom.com/wiki/Indrid_Cold
7. The Saucer Life - A Cold Day in West Virginia
8. The Inhumanoids - Barton M. Nunnelly: Page 183
9. Strange Creatures from Time and Space - John Keel: Page 182
10. The Mothman Prophecies - John Keel

Bibliography

Nessie's Exorcism

1. http://www.lochnessinvestigation.com/FSR.html
2. https://nocturnalrevelries.com/2020/04/12/the-goblin-universe-ted-holiday/
3. https://www.strangehistory.net/2014/04/24/nessie-as-biker-and-the-exorcism-of-the-loch/
4. https://en.wikipedia.org/wiki/Fredrick_William_Holiday
5. World Famous UFOs - Colin Wilson: Page 107
6. The Real Men in Black - Nick Redfern: Page 80
7. The Last Podcast On The Left - Episode 455

Printed in Dunstable, United Kingdom

76914366R00097